Akinbowale Isaac Adewumi

END TIME EVENTS

Christian eschatological views

WORKBOOK PRESS LLC
187 E Warm Springs Rd,
Suite B285, Las Vegas, NV 89119, USA

Website: https://workbookpress.com/
Hotline: 1-888-818-4856
Email: admin@workbookpress.com

Ordering Information:
Quantity sales. Special discounts are available on quantity purchases by corporations, associations, and others.
For details, contact the publisher at the address above.

Library of Congress Control Number:

ISBN-13:   978-1-960752-30-7 (Paperback Version)
             978-1-960752-31-4 (Digital Version)

REV. DATE: 03/20/2023

END TIME EVENTS

Christian Eschatological Views

Akinbowale Isaac Adewumi

Scripture quotations are taken from the HOLY BIBLE, KING JAMES VERSION (KJV)

Editing and inner text design layout:
Taiwo Adeodu +234 810 867 3939

DEDICATION

To the faithful fathers in the Lord - God's Generals.
"And shall come forth; they that have done good, unto the resurrection of life; and they that have done evil, unto the resurrection of damnation" (John 5:29).

CONTENTS

PREFACE

T he word, Eschatology, is a branch of study within Christian theology that derives its name from the Greek word *eschaton* and *logos*, the study of what the Bible says is going to happen in the end times. The study about the end of humans and the entire universe or the final judgement of all things and the destiny of humanity. It's very interesting to know that the Lord God Almighty, Who created all things for His glory, did not leave man in the dark about what is about to happen as well.

The Book of Amos 3:7 stated that "Surely the Lord God will do nothing, but he revealeth his secret unto his servants the prophets." After humanity fell out of a relationship with God, the Lord God of mercy began to unfold His plan to restore His holiness among His people through our Lord Jesus Christ.

The future prophecies of what is about to happen, the destiny of human souls and the end of the entire created order are made known to us in both the Old and New Testaments. "But thou, O Daniel, shut up the words, and seal the book, even to the time of the end: many shall run to and fro, and knowledge shall be increased" (Daniel 12:4).

Our scriptural knowledge is incomplete if we are destitute of the plan and will of God, most especially, the prophetic events that are ahead of us such as the rapture of the saints, the resurrection of the dead, the great tribulation, the second coming of Christ, the millennial reign, the great white throne judgment, the new heaven and new earth; and hell, the destiny of the wicked.

Moreover, the ubiquitous activities of false prophets on a rampage has led many people into deception through their false signs and wonders. It is interesting that the antichrist, who is the evil genius lurking behind the scenes, being the man of sin, will soon be revealed to fulfil his nefarious role accordingly.

Generally, the Bible has many references pointing to the end times, but only God knows the time specificity when these foreboding events will roll out. It only serves as a warning to all inhabitants of the earth that the end is imminent. We need to prepare to meet the Lord to avoid inescapable dangers associated with the end times as espoused by eschatology.

As a result, the true believer needs to carry out daily self-examination in the light of eternity through the mirror of God's word to see to it that he's walking righteously with Master Jesus and remain on his duty post preaching the gospel of Christ to the ends of the earth till the world knows about the Saviour Jesus.

Biblical eschatology has drawn much attention in the Christian faith because God loves to reveal His plans to

His prophets beforehand. As stated in Amos 3:7, this revelation guides our steps and motivates our lifestyle and active service in the vineyard of the Lord. During the earthly ministry of Jesus, the disciples asked, "...tell us, when shall these things be" (Mark 13:4). In the book of Mark 13:5-37; Mathew 24:4-12). Our Lord Jesus, in response to their question, gave cautions and admonitions which were needful with reference to the events that should come to pass.

Unequivocally, Jesus gave hints on deceivers and false Christs, the noise of wars, nation rise against nation, and kingdom against kingdom, intense persecution of brethren, climatic changes, earthquakes in diverse places, environmental hazards, famines and troubles, pestilences, love of God waxing cold in many believers, lawlessness, injustice, the trial of faith, tribulation, hatred, maliciousness, betrayal, untold suffering, an abomination of desolation, the emergence of a recessive world economy, carelessness and the need for all to watch.

Obviously, almost all events across the world, no doubt, have continued to confirm that the world is running its full course to drop its worn-out garment of rebellious act, unrighteousness, disobedience and sin against God. Hence, nobody can claim ignorance of the recent happening across the globe, all confirming earlier predictions and prophecies from the prophets that the second coming of our Lord Jesus Christ is at hand.

The Bible lifts the curtains and gives us a picture of some of the fearful events that will happen after the saints of God have been raptured, caught-up or taken home to be with the Lord actually. Although, many church assemblies or religious circles may give different interpretations to events of the end times, the fact remains that no true believer should go through the agony of end time events. The gory experiences, untold sufferings and fierce judgements are better imagined.

The reign of the antichrist will reach its height at this time and he will mobilise the world to fight against our Lord and Saviour Jesus Christ and the saints. Nevertheless, God, in His infinite power, will pour out His fierce judgment upon the people on the face of the earth during that time. There will be no hidden place for sinners, backsliders, religious infidels, proselytes, atheists and all who reject the gospel of salvation that the Lord brought for all men. The suffering and anguish will be too much to the point that men will still blaspheme God rather than repent. It would be too late to repent at this time because the Holy Ghost that could bring conviction upon people would have been withdrawn. Reader, don't get caught up in the coming battle and the outpouring of God's wrath upon the inhabitants of the earth.

Meanwhile, the essence of eschatology is to instill hope in times of troubles and trials to continue in godliness, righteousness and holiness of life. It's also to warn of the impending judgement awaiting sinners and backsliders. "Then said he to the multitude that came forth to be baptized of him, O generation of vipers, who hath warned you to flee from the wrath to come? Bring forth, therefore, fruits worthy of repentance, and begin not to say within yourselves, we have Abraham to our father: for I say unto you, That God is able of these stones to raise up children unto Abraham" (Luke 3:7-8). There's eternal punishment and separation from God's presence and Kingdom for those who refused to repent of their sins and accept Jesus Christ as Lord and personal Saviour. It's imperative for every Bible-believing Christian to embark on vigorous evangelism as commanded by the Lord.

Furthermore, it is significant to know that the sixty-nine weeks of Daniel's seventy-weeks of prophecy have come to pass. It remains a week for everything to come to an end. Since God has a plan for the Gentile nations, the stage we are now at is the Church age, which will be over after the rapture. The imminent second return of Christ doesn't mean that no there is no other biblical prophecies to be fulfilled before Christ returns. Yes! The God of salvation has a plan for the Gentile world. "And they shall fall by the edge of the sword, and shall be led away captive into all nations: and Jerusalem shall be trodden down of the Gentiles until the times of the Gentiles be fulfilled... For so hath the Lord commanded us, saying, I have set thee to be a light of the Gentiles, that thou shouldest be for salvation unto the ends of the earth" (Luke 21:24: Acts 13:47).

It is God's expectation from all believers to hold the fort by watching and praying.

In summary, the significance of eschatology to the nation of Israel is seen as the future tragedy that would befall the children of Israel (called the great tribulation or the time of Jacob's trouble - Jeremiah 30:7) due to their outright disobedience and rebellious attitude to God's covenant, will and purpose. The aftermath of this trouble will bring reconciliation, renewal and full restoration of God's purpose for the Jews.

In like manner, the Church will be consummated during the rapture. An understanding of Eschatology should eliminate many of the fears we have about the future and strengthen our faith in Christ. However, the careless Christians, backsliders and sinners that would be left behind during the Rapture shall witness the Great Tribulation. In this time of grace, it behoves us to work out our salvation with fear and trembling. The coming of the Lord is at hand!

I

Chapter 1

DANIEL'S PROPHECY OF SEVENTY WEEKS

The "seventy weeks" prophecy of Daniel is one of the most significant eschatological studies in which majority of the prophecies have been fulfilled. It provides the glimpses into Messianic prophecies from the Old Testament and the end time events. In Daniel chapter 9, Daniel humbly prayed and interceded for the nation of Israel by acknowledging their sins and trespasses against God and pleading for God's mercy.

In the process, Angel Gabriel appeared to him with revelation of what will happen to Israel soon. In Daniel's prophecy of 70 weeks, only a week is yet to be completed as 69 weeks have been fulfilled already. Let's go into the details of Daniel's prophecy of 70 weeks.

"Seventy weeks are determined upon thy people and upon thy holy city, to finish the transgression, and to make an end of sins, and to make reconciliation for iniquity, and to bring in everlasting righteousness, and to seal up the vision and prophecy, and to anoint the most Holy. Know therefore and understand, that from the going forth of the commandment to restore and to build Jerusalem unto the Messiah the Prince shall be seven weeks, and threescore and two weeks: the street shall be built again, and the wall, even in troubulous times. And after threescore and two weeks shall Messiah be

cut off, but not for himself: and the people of the prince that shall come shall destroy the city and the sanctuary; and the end thereof shall be with a flood, and unto the end of the war desolations are determined. And he shall confirm the covenant with many for one week: and in the midst of the week, he shall cause the sacrifice and the oblation to cease, and for the overspreading of abominations he shall make it desolate, even until the consummation, and that determined shall be poured upon the desolate (Daniel 9:24-27).

The revelation came to Daniel from God through the angel Gabriel in response and answer to Daniel's prayers because of the apostasy of the children of Israel. The focus of the prophecy above is centered on the nation of Israel and the city of Jerusalem. This prophecy is remarkable because it sets up the timing of both the first and second advents of our Lord and Saviour Jesus Christ. The seventy weeks is best described as 'seventy weeks of the years.' The Hebrew interpretation and translation for 'a week' is 'seven' while "weeks" is referred to as the word, "sevens."

The opening words of most English translations are "seventy weeks are determined." A week in the prophecy of Daniel means seven years; therefore, seventy weeks would be a total of 490 years. Angel Gabriel explained to Daniel that the following, as highlighted below, will happen during these seventy weeks prophecy:

The finish of the transgression: This refers to the children of Israel and their apostatic rejection of God. The act of rebellion and profanity of the Jews will come to an end as Jesus paid the price in full at Calvary (Matthew 23:37-39).

Making an end of transgression: This is the sin of dishonesty, an outright disobedience to God's word that will not last long, but come to an end by Jesus' vicarious death (Jeremiah 44:16-17).

Making atonement for iniquity: The blood of Jesus Christ shed for the sins of the whole world will become efficacious to actualize the redemption of Jews also when they would accept Jesus Christ as their Messiah at His second coming.

Bringing in everlasting righteousness: Certainly, the establishment of Christ's government on earth in the Millennial Reign will eliminate iniquity, transgression and sin of all kinds to usher in the new dispensation of Jesus' government of peace, righteousness, and justice.

Sealing up the vision and prophecy: The sealing up of vision and prophecy at this point is that the fulfilment would be at the end of seventieth week of Daniel's prophecy. At the end of seventieth week, God's divine Kingdom and the fulfilment of His holy covenants will come to pass. Also, the Jews that humiliated Jesus Christ at His first appearance will accept His Lordship over them and Christ would be glorified (1 Peter 1:11).

Anointing the most holy: This might be the anointing of the holiest temple devoted to God in the nearest future. In Matthew 24:14-16, there shall be a preceding abomination of desolation as the sign of Christ's second coming. I believe that there shall be the restoration of true worship in the temple when Jesus returns.

The seventy weeks of Daniel's prophecy are clearly demarcated into three while the period of the great tribulation falls within Daniel's seventieth week. There are 7 weeks or 49 years for rebuilding Jerusalem (Daniel 9:25), 62 weeks or 434 years from the completion of the building of Jerusalem to the end of the 49 years to the time the Messiah shall be revealed and the last or seventieth week of the last seven years which has also been divided into two periods.

The prophecy says that the starting point of 70 weeks of years will be the "decree to restore and rebuild Jerusalem." It is significant to know that the children of Israel were in captivity and Jerusalem was in ruins through Nebuchadnezzar. Sixty-nine weeks (483 years) were to transpire between the order to rebuild Jerusalem (after the Babylonian captivity) and the first advent of the Messiah.

In the seven weeks or forty-nine years, Jerusalem was to be reconstructed again, at the end of the sixty-two weeks or 434 years, the Messiah would be cut off (die or be crucified). This prophecy was exactly fulfilled. From 445 BC (Nehemiah 2:1-5) when Artaxerxes issued a decree concerning the rebuilding of the city of Jerusalem and as an answer to Nehemiah's request up until the end of the public advent of Christ the Messiah was 487 years.

In like manner, it was prophesied that the wicked prince that shall come shall destroy the city of Jerusalem. This happened in 70 A.D. when Roman soldiers under the leadership of General Titus invaded Jerusalem. Recall that Jesus' words of prophecy in this regard which states that, "...*verily, I say unto you, There shall not be left here one stone upon another, that shall not be thrown down*" (Matthew 24:2) was fulfilled to the letter.

This happened when the soldiers of Titus split up the gold-gilded temple stones piece-by-piece in search of gold trapped in-between each stone which they stripped carefully as treasured booty of war that they carted away. Hence no stone was left upon another. That's awesome! It's amazing how Bible prophecies get fulfilled with accuracy and precision! Many times, people and factors around the fulfillment of prophecies are oblivious of the significance of their roles.

Sixty-nine weeks of Daniel's seventy-weeks prophecy have been fulfilled while the last week is yet to be fulfilled. It's the Church age that intervenes in the time of the Messiah being cut off. This present dispensation of the church age was not directly predicted by the prophet in the Old Testament.

The Church age is a mystery according to Ephesians 3:5-6, "Which in other ages was not made known unto the sons of men, as it is now revealed unto his holy apostles and prophets by the Spirit; That the Gentiles should be fellow heirs, and of the same body, and partakers of his promise in Christ by the gospel." Therefore, this church age will be terminated by the Rapture. It is the rapture that will usher in Daniel's seventieth week, which is the period of the great tribulation and the revelation of the Antichrist.

The period of the great tribulation will be the darkest era in the history of mankind. The man of sin will be revealed and at this time, sin and evil will be highly celebrated, shamelessly permitted and strongly promoted. Before the rapture takes place, every believer in Christ is commanded by the Lord (Mark 16:15-16) to engage in vigorous evangelism and soulwinning to help sinners and backsliders before it's too late.

II

Chapter 2

THE MYSTERY OF THE CHURCH AGE

Church age is in-between the 69th and 70th weeks of Daniel's prophecy. The present church age remains a mystery of all ages to man because it was not revealed to any prophet in the Old Testament. Many prophets in the Old Testament predicted the two advents of Christ without any idea of the church era. God's own program for this dispensation called the "Church" didn't come by chance, it's significant because it was known to Him from the foundation of the world (Acts 15:18). "

"And to make all men see what is the fellowship of the mystery, which from the beginning of the world hath been hid in God, who created all things by Jesus Christ" (Ephesians 3:9; Please, read Ephesians 3:1-12). We learned from the verse of this Scripture that revealed to us that God's plans are unreachable, immeasurable and beyond human comprehension. In His wisdom, He often unveils them in His own time and to whom He wills. This mystery that was hidden from the days of Abraham, when he called him in Genesis 12:1-3, has been made available to us to become co-heirs with the descendants of Abraham.

The church age started with the Apostles and Jewish followers of our Lord Jesus Christ who spread the gospel message to the Jews, then to the whole world. This is the mystery that the Gentiles should be fellow heirs and of the same body; and partakers of His promise in Christ by the gospel (Ephesians 3:6). In other words, the gospel of salvation is not limited to the Jews, but to every race, color and in all geographical locations of the whole earth.

Paul, the apostle to the Gentiles, was especially privileged by God to have the revelation of this mystery of the dispensation of grace. "Whereof I am made a minister, according to the dispensation of God which is given to me for you, to fulfill the word of God; Even the mystery which hath been hidden from ages and from generations, but now is made manifest to his saints: To whom God would make known what are the riches of the glory of this mystery among the Gentiles; which is Christ in you, the hope of glory" (Colossians 1:25-27).

Prior to this time, there was a separation between the Jews and the Gentiles, this line of demarcation was broken down by the power of the gospel of Christ to make the Gentile nations partakers of divine nature and to have an inheritance among the saints. This gospel has made both the Jews and Gentiles joint heirs with the Son, Jesus Christ and the children of the Kingdom of God. It is significant to know that Christians, today, do not only know the mystery kept secret from saints of old, but indeed, the mystery is revealed!

In the same vein, the good Lord can still reveal His secret, the deep things of the Kingdom to the committed, consecrated and selfless believers who have found grace in His presence. The primary responsibility of the church saved by grace is to serve. We are commissioned to go into all the world and preach the gospel of Christ to every creature more than ever. Yes! We are saved to serve.

Chapter 3

SIGNS OF THE END TIME

End time is generally referred to as this present era and the commencement of the next dispensation in God's timetable. The great God does not only know the beginning of everything, He is the God of all knowledge Who knows the end of everything in this world. The hood of ignorance hanging over men on the surface of the earth makes it impossible for them to know just exactly what is coming next, how it may come and the best way to prepare against it.

Man is just like flowers that blossom in the morning with life's fragrance, but everything that glitters become gloomy when sunset comes. However, the God of all knowledge is fully aware of everyone's last moment on earth. This truth should bring us closer to God through genuine repentance of sins and reconciliation to learn from the gospel and prepare for the imminent. We are in the end times; the signs are all over us.

Only the gospel of Christ can empower us with the knowledge of the signs of the end times. "And as he sat upon the mount of Olives, the disciples came unto him privately, saying, tell us, when shall these things be? and what shall be the sign of thy coming, and of the end of the world?" (Matthew 24:3).

In response to the question that Christ's disciples asked, Christ warned them on what they should watch out against because it's a period when human survival would again be on the line like the time of Noah.

To summarise this in advance, the signs of the end times would include religious deception, wars, rumours of war, famines, pestilences, earthquakes in diverse places, intense persecution of followers of Christ, lawlessness, love of many waxing cold, running to and fro, upheavals, increase in knowledge, the doctrine of the devils (1 Timothy 4:1), false apostles (Revelation 2:2) and the rise of antichrist among others. Please, read Matthew 24.

Religious deception (verse 4-5). Christ warned that religious deception will be a major issue as the world approached the second coming of Jesus Christ. False Christs, false prophets, false teachers (2 Peter 2:1) and false brethren (2 Corinthians 11:26) are the order of the day this end time. These deceivers and their father, the devil, are out there to pervert the ways of the truth and beguile the true followers of Christ. These would be the enemies of the body of Christ in the end times, the only way out is to yield to Christ's warning by keeping our hearts diligently, remaining alert and searching the Scriptures (God's word) for guidance and prayers.

Wars and rumours of war (verse 6-7). The technological advancement of the 21st century, information technology with high-speed internet to disseminate information at high speed, the nuclear weapons, projectiles, rocket propellers, missiles, bombing devices and nanotechnology developed by many countries, have set the stage for world wars to take place at any time. There is a prevalence of infighting among the ethnic and religious nationals, political uprising, genocide and xenophobia.

The emergence of nuclear weapons of powerful nations, threats and intimidation are clear indications that this world is no more a secure place for mankind. Events around us show without any shadow of a doubt that we are in the end time. Consider the wars and rumours of wars, earthquakes, pestilences, epidemics, famines bedevilling the world (Matthew 24:4-8). Events that would have taken some past generations a couple of years to happen, now occur daily. Warfare is growing in sophistication and number.

Gone are the days of only physical warfare. Now, we hear of chemical, biological, atomic, nuclear and psychological warfare. Warfare now spans the whole of human life from the domestic to the global. Domestic warfare results in escalating divorces, broken homes, suicides and murders in the nuclear family unit; tribal warfare leads to ethnic-cleansing, genocide, national, international and global warfare.

Man has become a terror to himself. Nuclear warheads and ballistic missiles are positioned as if to announce the coming of doomsday! Spiritually, too, things are intensifying. Spiritual warfare is becoming fiercer, tenser and more deadly. The ignorant and the timid will fall as casualties in the battle (2 Corinthians 2:11; Hosea 4:6; Isaiah 5:13).

However, it is important for us to know that we can win the end time warfare. We shouldn't allow these to alarm us because "the end is not yet" because these things must happen first as events of the end time. Believers can also rest assured in the ever-abiding presence of the Most-high, His protection and sufficiency, irrespective of the troubles, challenges and fears in the world.

Famines (verse 7). There are going to be worldwide famines that will consume the land. The occurrence of famines is on the increase with currencies losing value, failing world economies, malnutrition and high death rates that have claimed millions of lives. This is the beginning of sorrows as stated by our Lord Jesus Christ, but believers should comfort themselves daily with God's word which has power and is still much relevant and at work even in these last days.

Pestilences (verse 7). These are epidemics and pandemics. The world has witnessed diseases and pandemics that claim millions of lives. Recently, coronavirus started spreading at the end of 2019 and was declared by the World Health Organisation (WHO) in March 2020. In West Africa, the world witnessed Ebola in 2014, Middle East Respiratory Syndrome (MERS) struck the Arabians Peninsula in 2014, and Zika virus in the Americas around 2016. Severe Acute Respiratory Syndrome (SARS), hantavirus, dengue, swine flu, West Nile virus, HIV/AIDS, influenzas, typhoid, measles and smallpox. All these have claimed untimely deaths of millions of lives. These also are the beginning of sorrows.

Earthquakes in divers' places (verse 7; Luke 21:11). It is the vibrations of the earth's crust that cause the earth's surface to shake or tremble causing destruction to cities and nations. Haiti, New Zealand, Japan, Chile, Nepal, and China have the reality of these devastating disasters that have claimed millions of lives and set nations economically backward. Hence, Christ describes it as "great earthquakes in diverse places" (Luke 21:11).

Earthquakes in the last one hundred years outnumber those recorded for the rest of human history. The good news is that no person living today must go through these horrible judgments that are awaiting the world if such accept Jesus Christ as Lord and personal Saviour today. We are in the church age, the era of "good tidings of great joy which shall be to all people"

Moreover, there's going to be the final, catastrophic upheaval, resulting in the destruction of the world as stated in the book of Revelation. Further, the earthquake is in second place a sign of the final judgment of God at the end of time. According to Revelation 16:18, "And there were voices, and thunders, and lightnings; and there was a great earthquake, such as was not since men were upon the earth, so mighty an earthquake, and so great" would take place at the very end of time in connection with the battle of Armageddon.

Iniquity shall abound (verse 12). This is outright disobedience and rejection of God's will and commandments and the substitution of self-will by not working in the Spirit, but in the flesh. We are in the last days and the spirit of the last is already working in so many lives today. "I charge thee therefore before God, and the Lord Jesus Christ, who shall judge the quick and the dead at his appearing and his kingdom; Preach the word; be instant in season, out of season; reprove, rebuke, exhort with all long-suffering and doctrine. For the time will come when they will not endure sound doctrine; but after their own lusts shall they heap to themselves teachers, having itching ears" (1 Timothy 4:1-3).

Due to the high rate of lawlessness, wickedness, intense persecution and treachery of false brethren, the love of many Christians towards God has reduced. This has resulted in selfishness, lethargy, self-serving, apostacy and such like the case of Demas who forsook Paul the apostle for the love of the things of this world (2 Timothy 4:10). Glory to God Almighty Who has made grace abound much more than sin through our Lord Jesus Christ! For believers to escape the horror of end-time sins, such must abound in the grace of God daily by searching the Scriptures and obeying it by grace and prayers. God's grace in you will make you overcome daily and live victoriously.

Increase in Knowledge (verse 12). The rapid increase in knowledge in is one of the end-time signs prophesied by Daniel in the Old Testament. "...many shall run to and fro, and knowledge shall be increased." We are living in 'The Information Technology Age' making this sign seem even more obvious as we daily experience increasing knowledge of science, diverse technology, medicine, travel and online commerce. (Please, read Daniel 12:4; Amos 8:11). We are living in the last days of a fast-paced world of computers, skills and surfing the internet, where young people are dazzled with new inventions, high-tech video games, digital economy and research for innovative ideas that have turned the world to a global village. All these are pointing us to the end times and imminent second coming of Christ Be prepared!

The abomination of desolation "And this gospel of the kingdom shall be preached in all the world for a witness unto all nations; and then shall the end come. When ye, therefore, shall see the abomination of desolation, spoken of by Daniel the prophet, stand in the holy place, (whoso readeth, let him understand:) Then let them which be in Judaea flee into the mountains:" (Matthew 24:15-16). Again, Lord Jesus Christ spoke about the event of "abomination of desolation" in the Olivet discourse as He referenced the prophetic event found in the book of Daniel (Daniel 9:27; 12:11), an end time sign, before His return to the earth.

An abomination is something that is detestable and would take place in the Israeli temple someday, that is, destroying and desecrating the holy place and leaving it in a horrible situation (Daniel 11:31-32). When this happens, it is a sign of Christ's imminent return. The abomination of desolation has three phases; two of these had been fulfilled and the remaining one is about to come to fulfillment. This prediction of Daniel about the future can briefly be explained as follows:

A future tyrant ruler will make a treaty with the children of Israel. The term of the agreement is a week of Daniel's prophecy, which is seven years. In the middle of the seven years, this tyrant leader will break the agreement and put an end to the sacrifices. This leader will desecrate the temple with sacrilege. The period of the desecration of the temple shall last for three and half years (1,290 days).

The first fulfillment of the abomination of desolation described the events that occurred in Jerusalem between 168/167 B.C. during the reign of terror of Antiochus

Epiphanes (8th Seleucid king Antiochus iv). He slaughtered great numbers of Jews and others were taken into slavery. The second fulfillment of the abomination of desolation occurred in 70 A.D. when Roman armies under General Titus took over Jerusalem. They destroyed the temple building and altar. "And when ye shall see Jerusalem compassed with armies, then know that the desolation thereof is nigh" (Luke 21:20). The Temple has been left desolate since that day; it has not been rebuilt.

In context, Our Lord Jesus Christ was speaking about the signs of the end and stated further that when you see the abomination of desolation spoken by Prophet Daniel, it is an event to occur in the future. Shortly after the abomination of desolation, there will be Great Tribulation (Read Matthew 24:16-21). In these verses, our Lord Jesus was referring to the antichrist, a satanic personality that will emerge in the end times to establish a covenant with the children of Israel for a period of one week (seven years) and break it in the middle (3½ years) to desecrate the rebuilt temple like what Antiochus Epiphanes did in the temple.

IV

Chapter 4

THE RAPTURE OF THE SAINTS

"Behold, I shew you a mystery; We shall not all sleep, but we shall all be changed, In a moment, in the twinkling of an eye, at the last trump: for the trumpet shall sound, and the dead shall be raised incorruptible, and we shall be changed. For this corruptible must put on incorruption, and this mortal must put on immortality. So when this corruptible shall have put on incorruption, and this mortal shall have put on immortality, then shall be brought to pass the saying that is written, Death is swallowed up in victory. O death, where is thy sting? O grave, where is thy victory?" (1 Corinthians 15:51-55. Please, read 1 Thessalonians 4:13-18).

God's prophetic clock is ticking to unfold this panoramic end-time program known as the rapture of the saints which is the greatest event of all ages that the Church (Ecclesia) is waiting for. It's the catching away of the saints from the earth, that is, all living saints and all who died in the Lord. "Saints" (Read Romans 1:7; 1 Corinthians 1:2; Colossians1:2 and Ephesians 1:1) are being mentioned here because Christ is coming for a glorious, holy church. True believers are constantly called saints because they are saved through the atoning blood of Jesus Christ and are daily living an overcoming life.

Apparently, the Old Testament prophets including Daniel did not see or know God's special programme for the Church. They only saw as far as the Messiah was cut off (or crucified) and the Millennium; they never saw the Church up until her Rapture. The parable of the Wise and Foolish Virgins is a food for thought.

The next event on God's time-table is the Rapture which is a Pre-tribulation event. There is no need to doubt the rapture because if Jesus came the first Time as Isaiah 7:14; 9:6-7 prophesied 600 years earlier, He will not delay His coming the second time as He Himself had said in John 14:1-3; Habakkuk 2:3. Look at it this way:

What is the Rapture? – The Catching away of Christ's saints (1 Thessalonians 4:16).
When is the Rapture? – No one knows the date (Mark 13:32).
Whom is the Rapture for? – Jesus' saints only are the candidates (Ephesians 5:27).
Where will the Rapture hold? – In the sky (1 Thessalonians 4:16-17).
Which way or how will the Rapture happen? – In the twinkling of an eye (1 Thessalonians 4:16-17).

Actually, the word **'Rapture'** is derived from the Latin word **'Rapio'** which means **'Caught up.'** In the same vein, however, Rapture means ecstatic departure of Christ's Church comprising both living and dead Saints to Heaven (I Thessalonians 4:13-18). The Pre-Tribulation Rapture is what the Bible teaches. The Scriptures describe two separate and distinct future events both of which are often confused. One is the first phase of Christ's second coming called the Pre-Tribulation Rapture of the Church when Christ Jesus comes **for** His saints to take His Bride, the Church home to be with Him (Revelation 3:11; 22:7, 12, 20) before the seven years Great Tribulation of Antichrist rule on earth begins (2 Thessalonians 2:1-12).

It is seen to be a description of a near-future preliminary event to the return of Christ described in Matthew 24:29-31. It is called the Pre-Trib Rapture, Pre-Trib Rapturo or the Pre-Trib Caught up. The Church will not escape temporary tribulation (Jn 16:33; 2 Corinthians 4:17) but will escape The Great Tribulation (Romans 5:9; I Thessalonians 1:10). The Rapture is NOT a Mid-Tribulation or Post Tribulation event.

A convincing typology of the Rapture is seen in both the Old and New Testaments. There are two examples of this in the Old Testament. In Genesis 5:24, the Bible records the translation of Enoch by physical disappearance without dying. It says, *"And Enoch walked with God: and he was not; for God took him."* This is corroborated in Hebrews 11:5. Furthermore, Prophet Elijah did not see death after the completion of his ministry and the vicarious commissioning of Prophet Elisha, but was literally transported by *a chariot of and horses of fire* from earth into Heaven. This is God's

Rocket before physicists' developed present-day rockets (2 Kings 2:1, 11-12).

Two instances that confirm the reality of the Rapture in the New Testament are cited hereunder. The first is the physical Ascension of Christ into Heaven in the clear view of His disciples with angelic certification in Acts 1:9-11. Secondly, dead saints were raised/resurrected (Not Reincarnated) after the Resurrection of Jesus Christ and visited their loved ones in Matthew 27:51-53. By extension, a shadow of this same type was when Evangelist Philip was also divinely transported too from Gaza and was found at Azotus in Acts 8:31).

Interestingly, the Bible clearly teaches that the second phase of Christ's second coming is the Post-Rapture coming of Christ in the clouds **with** His RAPTURED SAINTS to rule literally on earth for one thousand years or Millennium (Jude 1:14-15). On the flip side, however, there will be a Post-Tribulation Resurrection for Tribulation Saints who refuse to take the mark of the beast in Revelation 7:13-14. It is also known as the second resurrection. Hints on our preparation (Read 1 Thessalonians 5:1-10; 2 Peter 3:8-18; Revelation 21:27; 22:14-15). *"And there shall in no wise enter into it any thing that defileth, neither whatsoever worketh abomination, or maketh a lie: but they which are written in the Lamb's book of life."*

The story of the ten virgins in Matthew chapter 25 said it all. Five of them had enough oil in their lamps to keep them burning up until they see the Bridegroom face to face. In other words, Christ is not coming for a careless denomination member or churchgoer without salvation. He's coming for the Bible-believing Christians whose lives are being regulated by God's word. The Rapture of the saints which shall be heralded by Christ's appearance in the air at the trump of God is the first phase of Christ's second coming. Though the rapture is also generally and freely referred to as the second coming of Christ, it's an initial phase since Jesus Christ will merely appear in the air and rapture or catch up the ready saints.

The rapture will take place before the great tribulation when the wrath of God will be poured down from His cup of indignation without mixture upon the inhabitants of the earth when the Antichrist begins his reign of terror. It can happen anytime from now and saints of God are being encouraged to prepare daily.

The rapture, like the ultimate second coming of Christ, is imminent and certain. Immediately after the rapture, which is the first phase of Christ's second coming *for* His bride, there will be a seven-year period of Great Tribulation on earth while the seven-year Marriage Supper of the Lamb simultaneously happens in Heaven. The expiration of the seven-year period will usher in the second phase of Christ's second coming *with* the raptured saints for the Millennium which is Christ's 1,000 years literal reign on earth.

At the rapture, Christ will appear in the air and not all eyes will see Him, but only the redeemed of the Lord will partake of this as it will happen in the twinkle of an eye! Here, the mission of Christ is to resurrect all saints that died in the Lord, who, along with the living believers, will put on immortality and shall be caught up to be with Lord. At the second coming, the feet of Christ will rest on the mount called Olivet, and all eyes will see Him (Zechariah 14:4-11; Revelation 19:1-16).

However, the rapture is the present expectation of the saints. It is the next event in the program of God for the Church age. The time of the rapture is unknown, even by the angels (Mark 13:32). The rapture will be announced by the voice of the archangel and the blowing of trumpet signalling the end of the church age. The rapture was a mystery unknown to the Old Testament saints and the prophets. God had underscored this great event in two different ways in the Scripture to assure us of its certainty.

Firstly, it was illustrated in Enoch and Elijah, the two living saints who did not taste death, but were translated in a moment of time and caught up in the air (Genesis 2:24; 2 Kings 2:11-12). Secondly, it was illustrated by Christ in the New Testament, He died, was buried and resurrected. While He talked with His disciples on Mount Olivet, He was caught up and a cloud received Him out of their sight (Acts 1:9 -11).

The rapture which was a mystery to the Old Testament prophets marks the end of the church age, also referred to as the time of the Gentiles (Luke 21:24) This mystery was in the original plan of God for the Gentile nations, "known unto God are His works from the foundation of the earth" (Acts 15:18). In His mercy, by the interpolation of the church age, Christ the Messiah came for His people, but they rejected Him (John 1:11) therefore, God turned to the Gentiles to take a people for Himself. The rapture of the saints will mark the end of this special period of grace. Does this mean that God has forsaken His people in Israel forever? Far from it! God will resume His program with Israel immediately after the rapture, thus ushering in the beginning of the seventieth week of Daniel's prophecy (Daniel 9:24-27).

Any moment from now, the trumpet shall sound, and He that shall come will come and will not tarry. It is very sure and certain that our Lord Jesus Christ is coming back! He assured the church of the certainty of His coming (John 14:1-3). Angels of God proclaimed His coming and apostles and saints of all ages preached it. All the signs of His coming are daily being fulfilled. All the happenings in the world in fulfillment of the prophecies in the Scriptures confirm that the coming of the Lord is nearby.

Soon, the Lord shall appear in the sky and at the sound of the trumpet, the dead in Christ and the saints alive shall go to meet the Lord in the air. The wise that have extra oil in their lamps shall go in with the Bridegroom, but the careless and foolish shall cry, "Lord, Lord, open to us" and they shall be told, "I know you not!" Many shall, however, realise too late at the coming of the Lord that religion without regeneration, self-denial without salvation, good works without grace in the heart and fasting without faith in the atoning blood of Jesus Christ will not make them fit for the rapture.

The Lord is coming for the saints - those without spot or wrinkle - the holy ones without blemish (Hebrews 12:14-15). The purpose of His coming is to receive them so that where He is, they may be also. Take for instance, every wise person going on a journey prepares ahead of time, but the foolish will delay the processing of his travelling documents until the last minute. Such a person would miss their flight. We have no continuing city here as we have a short time to prepare for the coming of the Lord. If we do not want to be disappointed and left behind to go through the period of the great tribulation, this is the period to prepare and get ready.

Now, we still have time to pray for salvation, restoration, inner purity (sanctification) and settle differences (restitution) before the sound of the trumpet. The careless souls shall be left behind to suffer the same fate as the sinners under the rule of the antichrist. The sound of the trumpet marks the end of all troubles and sorrows for the beloved saints of God, but it also signifies the beginning of sorrow and anguish for unrepentant sinners and backsliders.

The saints shall be called up to partake in the marriage supper of the Lamb. We would be brought before the judgement seat of Christ for an examination. "And behold, I come quickly; and my reward is with me, to give every man according as his work shall be."

Our works shall be tested by fire before the promised rewards are given. "And the fire shall try every man's work of what sort it is." Some people will suffer loss; that is, loss of reward. Others will receive a reward. God has given us a heavenly pattern of godliness to follow to be able to meet the rapture.

A new creature in Christ through genuine salvation, washed in the blood of the Lamb, transformed by the Spirit of God, guided by His word and the personality of Christ, is to show himself a pattern of good works. "In all things shewing thyself a pattern of good works: in doctrine, showing no corruption, but gravity, sincerity, sound speech, that cannot be condemned; that he that is of the contrary part may be ashamed, having no evil thing to say of you" (Titus 2:7-8).

The Lord wants us to live an exemplary life of good behaviour with virtuous nature of true followers of Christ for others to emulate in the society. Just as the salt adds value and sweetens our foods, so also must Christians be a salt in the community. Our Christian journey begins with salvation and progress towards maturity and mastery. Therefore, we must always be

Christlike models who are controlled and guided by the Spirit of God in all things.

In all things, children (without age limit) must obey their parents. Servants must respect their masters, wives must be faithful and husbands must show true love. Saints who have tasted God's grace must live according to His will "that God in all things may be glorified."

Therefore, friends and readers, how are you preparing for this great event? Are you born again? Are your sins washed in the precious blood of Jesus? Come to the Lord today without delay. "Now is the day of salvation." Watch and pray daily for Christ's imminent second coming! Jesus is not coming a second time to die as a Lamb for sin or save sinners, but He is coming as the Lion to gather the repented sinners known as saints unto Himself and to judge this wicked world! Hence you need to get yourself prepared!

Chapter 5

MARRIAGE SUPPER OF THE LAMB

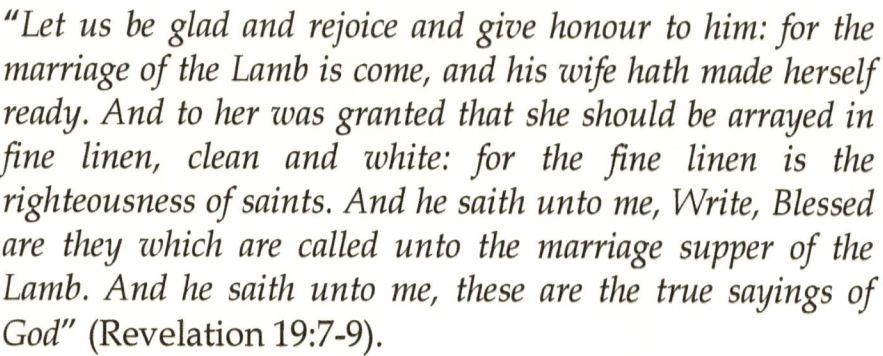

"Let us be glad and rejoice and give honour to him: for the marriage of the Lamb is come, and his wife hath made herself ready. And to her was granted that she should be arrayed in fine linen, clean and white: for the fine linen is the righteousness of saints. And he saith unto me, Write, Blessed are they which are called unto the marriage supper of the Lamb. And he saith unto me, these are the true sayings of God" (Revelation 19:7-9).

In the Scriptures, the great banquet of the Lord, after the rapture, is called the Marriage Supper of the Lamb. This is the banquet that consummates the Kingdom of Christ in celebrating the marriage of the Lamb to His bride whom He has made worthy of her husband. Sequel to this is the final defeat of the enemies of Christ. Meanwhile, Christ the Lamb of God is the Bridegroom, the King of kings, and the Lord of lords Who shed His precious blood to cleanse us from all our sins. His Bride is the Church of Jesus Christ, "…who hath made himself ready."

The church is adorned in fine white linen (the righteous acts of the saints) and the church is united to Christ in a glorious celebration. This calls for celebration because the stage is set for the long-awaited union of the marriage supper of the Lamb. The Church is the opposite of the soul-hunting Babylon who opposed everything that's good and holy. Babylon detests the things of God and always appeared flamboyant in her immodest dress. In the Old Testament Israel was described as the wife of The Lord who has been away because of her idolatries and adulteresses.

"For thy Maker is thine husband; the LORD of hosts is his name; and thy Redeemer the Holy One of Israel; The God of the whole earth shall he be called. For the LORD hath called thee as a woman forsaken and grieved in spirit, and a wife of youth, when thou wast refused, saith thy God. For a small moment have I forsaken thee; but with great mercies will I gather thee. In a little wrath I hid my face from thee for a moment; but with everlasting kindness will I have mercy on thee, saith the LORD thy Redeemer" (Isaiah 54:5-8).

Israel will be restored to the Lord, but no restored wife is ever referred to as a virgin. In the first instance, the church was betrothed to Christ at salvation during the present church age in watching and praying (2 Corinthians 11:2). Secondly, the coming Christ will take his bride (the church) from this present evil world through the rapture to His Father's house which He has prepared for them.

The Marriage Supper of the Lamb will take place in Heaven immediately after the rapture. In view of this, John the Baptist referred to himself as "the friend of the bridegroom" (John 3:29). Hence, the church, saved out of all languages, tribes, people, and nations, from among the Jews and Gentiles is the bride. She makes herself ready by being cleansed and washed in the blood of Christ, by abiding in Christ and "putting on the new man, which after God is created righteousness and true holiness" being clothed in the righteousness of the saints.

Old Testament saints will be guests at the Marriage Supper of the Lamb. (Luke 13:28-29; Revelation 6:9-11; 19:7-9). The Lord will be praised and adored by an innumerable crowd whom He has redeemed by His blood of every kindred, tongue, people and nation. This present dispensation of the church age will close with the rapture and the stage of the long-awaited celebration will commence with His people.

VI

Chapter 6

THE GREAT TRIBULATION

A critical look at the word *Tribulation*, which was first mentioned in the book of Deuteronomy 4:27-30 when Moses warned the children of Israel on their way to the Promised Land of the consequence of forsaking the Lord their God, indicated the judgments of God upon them. It clearly shows that they would be scattered among the nations. He prophesied that God would reserve mercy for them in the latter days and deliver them from the tribulation and take them into covenant with Himself.

The general tribulation is the common past and current persecution of believers and Jews over time as expressed by Jesus in John 16:33 where He specifically clarified it, saying, "These things I have spoken unto you, that in me ye might have peace. In the world ye shall have *tribulation*: but be of good cheer; I have overcome the world." The tribulation mentioned here is totally different from the Great Tribulation which will be elucidated here.

Our Lord Jesus Christ and the Apostles minced no words that there is going to be a tribulation different from the present general temporal and common phenomenon experienced virtually by all believers in form of ailments, natural disasters, global recession, wars, poverty, marital problems, martyrdom, terrorism and persecution from enemies of the cross and ungodly governments over time. (John 16:33; Matthew 24:6-20; Acts 5:41; 2 Corinthians 11:22-33; Philippians 1:29-30; 1 Peter 5:9; 4:12-16).

The future terrible period on earth after the Rapture is known as The Great Tribulation or the time of Jacob's trouble (Jer. 30:7). It is shortened to a 7 years rule of The Anti-Christ on earth (Ezekiel 4:6). It is also proximate to the Great Day of the Lord. (Joel 2:1-2, 31; Zephaniah 1:14-18; Malachi 4:5; Acts 2:20). Only those who reject the Mark of the Beast (Revelation 13:1-18) will be severely persecuted beyond measure and most of them executed, but they will be saved as Tribulation Saints when Jesus returns to earth with the Raptured Saints to establish the Millennium along with Old Testament saints too. (Revelation 7:13-17; 20:4-6).

During the Olivet Discourse, Jesus' prophecy found in Matthew 24:21-22 was made. "For then shall be **Great Tribulation**, such as was not since the beginning of the world to this time, no, nor ever shall be. And except those days should be shortened, there should no flesh be saved: but for the elect's sake those days shall be shortened." This is the most extensive of Christ's explanations of what will occur during the end times prior to His second coming. In like manner, Jeremiah 30:7 revealed that "Alas! for that day is great, so that **none is like** it: it is even the time of Jacob's trouble, but he shall be saved out of it."

The children of Israel will suffer in a greater measure than ever before to the point that the severity of their suffering will cause them to cry out in agony for their Messiah to come and deliver them. "And I will bring the third part through the fire, and will refine them as silver is refined, and will try them as gold is tried: they shall call on my name, and I will hear them: I will say, it is my people: and they shall say, The LORD is my God" (Zechariah 13:9). The dominant figure of the great tribulation will be the antichrist, a personal being with all sorts of satanic powers to govern the whole world at the time. The great tribulation will be the most awesome, horrible event in human history; a time of trouble indeed and will last for seven years (the last week of Daniel's prophecy of seventy weeks).

It will end at the second phase of the second coming of our Lord Jesus Christ when He alights on Mount Olives as discussed in Zechariah 14:4, "And his feet shall stand in that day upon the mount of Olives, which is before Jerusalem on the east, and the mount of Olives shall cleave in the midst thereof toward the east and toward the west, and there shall be a very great valley; and half of the mountain shall remove toward the north, and half of it toward the south."

Jesus will reign on earth from Jerusalem for a thousand years called the Millennial Reign (Revelation 20:4-5). The purpose of the great tribulation is to make the children of Israel suffer for their disobedient and rebellious attitude towards the God of the covenant so that they could cry to God and repent of their wilful transgressions against the Messiah Whom they rejected before He can come back to them.

At the same time, the unbelieving men and women of all ages will be judged during the great tribulation. It will be a period of unparalleled suffering, famines, dreadful woes, judgments, and great plagues will be sent upon the earth during this time. It will be a period of bloody wars, explosions, civil uprisings, terrorism, geographical upheavals, rending of the universe, pestilences, anguish, earthquakes, destruction and death. No one on earth will be able to buy, sell or earn income without submission to the dictates of the Antichrist. It will be a time that the inhabitants of the earth will be calling upon the mountains to fall upon them and hide them from the terror of the Lord. "And the kings of the earth, and the great men, and the rich men, and the chief captains, and the mighty men, and every bondman, and every free man, hid in the dens and in the rocks of the mountains; And said to the mountains and rocks, Fall on us, and hide us from the face of him that sixtieth on the throne, and from the wrath of the Lamb: For the great day of his wrath is come; and who shall be able to stand?" (Revelation 6:15-17).

The wrath of God will be poured out without mixture upon the inhabitants of this earth in a time of fear and terror, a period of torment beyond description and gross darkness indeed shall it be. Seas will be polluted;

cattle and vegetation will be destroyed and millions will be dying from catastrophes that will befall the earth.

As a matter of fact, a huge portion of the population of the earth will be destroyed. It's going to be a time of universal trouble with the epicenter in Jerusalem and Palestine according to Jeremiah 30:7. The antichrist that would enter into seven years peace covenant with Israel will break it in the middle (Three and half years) and attack Jerusalem with frightening wars, destruction and desolation (Revelation 11:1-19; Daniel 7:24-25). It's going to be "as a man did flee from a lion, and a bear met him; or went into the house, and leaned his hand on the wall, and a serpent bit him" (Amos 5:19). Animals in the bush and men will be in trouble; even mighty men will weep bitterly. "Neither their gold nor silver will be able to deliver them" at that time of the great tribulation.

The antichrist shall subdue nations under his reign of terror. The false prophet shall herald and popularize him, making men and women worship his image. During this time, no one can buy or sell without the mark or number (666) of the beast. As these things are happening on earth, the saints of God that have gone with Christ in the rapture will be receiving their rewards in Heaven (Revelation 11:25-28; 3:12).

VII

Chapter 7

TWO WITNESSES OF THE
GREAT TRIBULATION

"And there was given me a reed like unto a rod: and the angel stood, saying, Rise, and measure the temple of God, and the altar, and them that worship therein. But the court, which is without the temple leave out, and measure it not; for it is given unto the Gentiles: and the holy city shall they tread under foot forty and two months. And I will give power unto my two witnesses, and they shall prophesy a thousand two hundred and threescore days, clothed in sackcloth" (Revelation 11:1-3).

This event falls within the great tribulation period. The temple measured here is the temple in Jerusalem. The measuring depicts God's intention to possess the temple fully in the future and those who worship therein. It's meant to draw the children of Israel into a covenant with Him just as predicted by Daniel."

The court which is without the temple" will yet be dominated by the Gentiles for 42 months during the Great Tribulation (Please, read Revelation 11:1-18). During the days of the great tribulation, God will cause two mighty prophets to arise. These two prophets shall give a worldwide testimony of God's salvation and judgment. Both of them shall denounce the wickedness of the time.

Furthermore, the two witnesses are God's instruments representing the law and the prophets. Someone suggested that they will be Moses and Elijah, while others think they will be Enoch and Elijah. Those who identify them as Enoch and Elijah say that anyone who lives on earth must die to fulfill Hebrew 9:27 which says, "And as it is appointed unto men once to die, but after this the judgment."

However, there is going to be a whole generation that will never taste death according to 1 Corinthians 15:51-52) which says, "Behold, I shew you a mystery; We shall not all sleep, but we shall all be changed, In a moment, in the twinkling of an eye, at the last trump: for the trumpet shall sound, and the dead shall be raised incorruptible, and we shall be changed."

Therefore, the ministry and miracles of these will be like the ministries of Moses and Elijah, but the truth is that these future prophets are not identified or named here. Their ministry will last for three and half years that is, during the period of the second period of the great tribulation. Their dress of sackcloth shows them to be prophets in an evil age calling not for rejoicing but rather for mourning, repentance, and judgment.

In Revelation 11:4; and Exodus 27:20, The olive tree gives olive oil which was the fuel for the candle lights.

Thus, "these two olive trees and candlesticks symbolise those who are abundantly filled with God's Spirit. Their lives will be supernaturally protected during the period of their ministry on earth. Meanwhile, this time, the wicked see the terrifying events connected with the two witnesses and the world will be fearful as they behold the irrefutable power and glory of God.

In Revelation 11:7-10, God, in His own timing, does permit His prophets/ministers to exit the world when their ministry on earth is finished. The same thing will happen to the two witnesses that will overcome and get killed by the beast from the bottomless pit. Their bodies are a symbol of victory over the beast and those who oppose the purpose of God. Prior to this, the wicked will see their corpse as an occasion of great rejoicing to the point that they will have feasts and send gifts to one another.

In verses 11-12, the joy and celebration of those who rejoice over the death of the two witnesses were cut short when the two witnesses are resurrected to life. Yes! The triumphing of the wicked is short and the joy of the hypocrite is but for a moment (Job 20:5). Great fear will fall upon those who will see them as they stand on their feet. Their amazement will increase as a voice from heaven says to the witnesses, "Come up hither" as they watch them ascending to heaven. Within an hour of the ascension of God's two witnesses, there occurs a catastrophic earthquake.

Seven thousand men died immediately and the remnant become affrighted. As the seventh angel blows the seventh trumpet, mighty shout of acclamation and praise are lifted up to God. When the seventh trumpet is blown the heavenly citizens know that it contains the final decisive bowl of judgements. Shout for joy that, "the kingdom of this world becomes the kingdom of our Lord, and of His Christ, and He shall reign forever and ever." With the blowing of this seventh trumpet, God is clearly now, the Conqueror; the battle won though, it yet rages on earth; the joy is unspeakable!

Now, is time for every believer to embark on vigorous evangelism for the salvation of the people in the world because the God of the covenant will accomplish His word.

VIII

Chapter 8

THE ANTICHRIST: THE BEAST

L iterally speaking, the meaning of the term *antichrist* is simply "against Christ." The symbolic representation of key figure in the end times that will oppose anything that is called God. The antichrist is a personality who will rule the world just before the Second Coming of Jesus Christ. He will seek world domination and will attempt to destroy the nation of Israel and the followers of Jesus Christ. The diabolic power of the Antichrist will make him the idol of the world that will be demanded to be worshipped (Please, read Revelation 13:1-18).

"And in the latter time of their kingdom, when the transgressors are come to the full, a king of fierce countenance, and understanding dark sentences, shall stand up. And his power shall be mighty, but not by his own power: and he shall destroy wonderfully, and shall prosper, and practise, and shall destroy the mighty and the holy people. And through his policy also he shall cause craft to prosper in his hand; and he shall magnify himself in his heart, and by peace shall destroy many: he shall also stand up against the Prince of princes; but he shall be broken without hand...And the beast which I saw was like unto a leopard, and his feet were as the feet of a bear, and his mouth as the mouth of a lion: and the dragon gave him his power, and his seat, and great authority. And I saw one of his heads as it

were wounded to death; and his deadly wound was healed: and all the world wondered after the beast. And they worshipped the dragon which gave power unto the beast: and they worshipped the beast, saying, who is like unto the beast? who is able to make war with him?" (Daniel 8:23-25; Revelation 13:2-4).

There are many antichrists represented by Satanism, Atheism, Islam, Romanism, Buddhism, Hinduism, Illuminati and other religions outside of Christ (1 John 2:18, 22; 4:3; 2 John vs 7) but there is The Anti-Christ whose title synchronises with Revelation 13:1-18. The Anti-Christ is the king of fierce countenance, the scarlet prince, the electronic evil genius who will rule the world in terror for 7 years – Daniel 8:23. The antichrist will have a Jewish root/stock, but will rise to global prominence through diplomatic relations with Rome (2 Thessalonians 2:1-12).

In the Scriptures, the Antichrist is rightly described as the Beast (the beast rising from the sea will be a person, a man – Revelation 13:18) and rising up out of the sea of humanity (Isaiah 57:20). The antichrist is also identified as the king of the north, the king of Babylon, the Syrian, the Assyrian, the Extortioner, the man of sin, the little horn, the devil, the prince that shall come, a king of fierce countenance and understanding dark sayings, the spoiler, the man of perdition and that wicked one empowered personally by Satan. He is a ruler with great power, authority, dominion and authority. The heads and crowns of the beast represent multiplied regal power and the dominion that he possesses.

The Antichrist or the beast is a man who will be energised and empowered by Satan the Dragon to wage war against Christians and Israel and take over the world. The height of his description is that "...upon his head is the name of blasphemy." Here, the Scripture is making it clear to us about the main purpose of Satan which is to belittle the personality of the Holy Trinity and blaspheme the great name of God.

The position of the antichrist as the second personality in the unholy trinity, the kingdom of Satan (that is, Satan - the Dragon, the Antichrist – the first beast and the False prophet – the second beast). Satan called the dragon or devil, the supreme head of darkness, is going to delegate his authority and power to the antichrist like Jesus Christ has been given all the power in heaven and in the earth by God the Father (Matthew 28:18).

Since time immemorial, Satan has constantly rebelled against God in all things, he's anti-God and works against God's plan on earth. Through the antichrist, Satan is going to carry out the climax of his rebellious operations on earth. His reign of terror during the great tribulation will be ushered in by deception, flatteries, prosperity and a call for peace. Through his crafty method and the help of the false prophet, he will cause all men and women, both small and great, rich and poor that were not born again and careless believers also, to take the mark (666) of the beast. This seals the doom of whosoever receives this mark.

The beast resembles three animals – swift leopard like Greece, strong bear like Medo-Persia and fierce lion-like Babylon (Daniel 7:3-17). He will have all the attributes of the world rulers before him. This monster, the terrible creature, is a symbol of the last world political power that shall rule over the nations at the time of the end. "Who opposeth and exalteth himself above all that is called God, or that is worshipped; so that he as God sitteth in the temple of God, showing himself that he is God" (2 Thessalonians 2:4).

The Antichrist will present himself in God's position that would make all the inhabitants of the earth to adore and worship him. Unfortunately, the apostate church that is left behind will surrender to the government and control of the beast with those who do not believe in the gospel of Christ. In revelation 17:9-10, the beast is described as "seven kings." The five fallen ones are the five ancient empires that preceded the day of the Apostle John. Theses are the Egyptian, the Assyrian, the Babylonian, the Persian and the Greek empires. Then, "...and one is" means the empire in existence when the Apostle John lived and wrote – the Roman Empire. The one that is yet to come is the final political dominion of the Antichrist. His reign will begin immediately after the rapture of the saints.

Chapter 9

THE FALSE PROPHET: THE SECOND BEAST

"And I beheld another beast coming up out of the earth; and he had two horns like a lamb, and he spake as a dragon. And he exerciseth all the power of the first beast before him, and causeth the earth and them which dwell therein to worship the first beast, whose deadly wound was healed. And he doeth great wonders, so that he maketh fire come down from heaven on the earth in the sight of men, And deceiveth them that dwell on the earth by the means of those miracles which he had power to do in the sight of the beast; saying to them that dwell on the earth, that they should make an image to the beast, which had the wound by a sword, and did live" (Revelation 13:11-14).

E vidently, the false prophet is the third personality in the unholy trinity of Satan. As the Holy Trinity is characterised by love, infinite truth, righteousness and the goodness of God, so also is the unholy trinity of Satan that reveals the traits of deception, hatred and unadulterated evil which portrays the diametrically opposite of God's plan for the whole world.

Satan is the anti-God, the Beast is the anti-Christ and the False prophet is the anti-Spirit that would rule the world during the great tribulation (Please, read Revelation 13:11-18). The main work of the false prophet is to divert and direct the worship of the people on earth to the antichrist. Both beasts (Antichrist and the False prophet) portray a strong authoritative power and force that will conquer the nations of the world and persecute those who follow Christ.

Consequently, it's significant for all Bible-believing Christians to always be prepared and ready in order to be counted worthy to make it at the rapture. Those who are left behind after the rapture will cry, but their cries would be too late! The only alternative for them is to pass through the great tribulation period.

The second beast, who is the third member of the unholy trinity, will claim to have God's Spirit and speak on His behalf with great deception and lying wonders. Through his personality, he will exercise power, influence people, do great wonder before the people and deceive them that dwell on the earth. "He had two horns like a lamb, and he spake as a dragon."

This means that the beast will put on the appearance and calmness of a lamb to deceive many people, whereas, his true nature is the wickedness of the devil! Our Lord Jesus Who knows the heart of all men warned that false prophets would come "in sheep's clothing, but inwardly, they are ravenous wolves (Matthew 7:15).

It's very important to know that the purpose of the false prophet's miracles is not to deliver people from the present and eternal suffering to come, but to convince them enough to make them worship the first beast, thereby making men irredeemable servants, slaves and worshippers of Satan. Hence those who do not worship the image of Satan will the first beast put to death. This unholy trinity will persecute believers and the children of Israel and deceive many others, resulting in their eternal death, but God will prevail and His Kingdom on earth will stand.

"And the beast was taken, and with him the false prophet that wrought miracles before him, with which he deceived them that had received the mark of the beast, and them that worshipped his image. These both were cast alive into a lake of fire burning with brimstone" (Revelation 19:20). Whatever has a beginning will surely have an end and God will never allow evil to thrive for long because Satan only has a short time (three years and six months) to demonstrate his act of wickedness in fullness.

Therefore, the beast and the false prophet will be arrested and cast alive into a lake of fire burning with brimstone where unrepentant sinners of all ages will end up ultimately.

Chapter 10

MARK OF THE BEAST (666)

"And he causeth all, both small and great, rich, and poor, free and bond, to receive a mark in their right hand, or in their foreheads: And that no man might buy or sell, save he that had the mark, or the name of the beast, or the number of his name. Here is wisdom. Let him that hath understanding count the number of the beast: for it is the number of a man; and his number is Six hundred threescore and six" (Revelation 13:16-18).

Certainly, the mark of the beast will be an end-time identification mark (666) required on the right hand or on the forehead. It is an act of seal for the followers/worshippers of the Antichrist through the enticement of the false prophet (the spokesperson for the Antichrist) to be able to buy or sell. This event will be carried out in the whole world. The time and the stage are set and no one will be able to buy, sell and earn income on earth during the reign of the antichrist without the mark of the beast. It is still possible to buy or sell through cash, cheques, debit, or credit cards and through online payment such as PayPal, e-transfer (interac e-transfer), Amazon pay, Apple pay, Google pay, among other means.

Planting chips/barcodes in the hand or on the forehead are now possible. The vast possibilities in this age of information technology prepare the stage for the event. The mark of the beast on the forehead or right hand indicates that the one wearing it is a worshipper of the beast or signifies devotion, loyalty and submission to the rule of the beast. The people who refused to have the mark of the beast will be killed or starved to death. Although, the beast will have a short-lived grant of authority and power, God will allow the Antichrist to rule for 42 months.

At the end of those months, our Lord Jesus Christ will return, and Satan will wage war against Him to stop the Kingdom of peace that He comes to establish, but Satan and his cohorts will fail and be defeated. Therefore, the devil shall be bound for one thousand years. Christ will then establish His Millennial Kingdom on earth and His saints will return with Him. Finally, Satan will be released for a while after the thousand years and then be defeated and cast into the lake of fire and all his cohorts.

XI

Chapter 11

TRIBULATION SAINTS

"And when he had opened the fifth seal, I saw under the altar the souls of them that were slain for the word of God, and for the testimony which they held: And they cried with a loud voice, saying, how long, O Lord, holy and true, dost thou not judge and avenge our blood on them that dwell on the earth? And white robes were given unto every one of them; and it was said unto them, that they should rest yet for a little season, until their fellow servants also and their brethren, that should be killed as they were, should be fulfilled" (Revelation 6:9-11; Please, read the whole chapter 6).

Frankly speaking, the Holy Scriptures clearly revealed that a great multitude of both the Jews and Gentiles will trust in the Lord after the church has ascended via the rapture. These people who will come to faith in Jesus Christ during the great tribulation period are tribulation saints. During this time, the outpouring of the wrath of God will begin for the world. Things will get worse on earth because of the antichrist, the deceiver that would unleash his leadership of terror on the world before Christ the great Deliverer comes to establish a reign of peace on the reclaimed earth. With the rapture of the church, the age of grace gives way to the age of wrath and vengeance; the long period of grace comes to an end and a seven-year period of judgment and tribulation begins.

The seven-sealed scroll being opened by Christ contains the judgment of God on the world of sinners. As the seals are broken, a series of devastating judgments are released on the people on earth. The barking of the seals gradually reclaims the earth for Christ, the rightful owner of all things that were ever created. The first four seals make the world witness and experience false peace and false security, war, unprecedented bloodshed, famine, total economic collapse, pestilence and horrible deaths. In the first four seals, the restraining influence of the Holy Spirit is withdrawn and uncontrolled men bring evils and calamities to one another.

During the period of the first four seals, those who believe in Christ after the rapture of the church are killed in fierce persecution. They were killed "for the word of God and for the testimony which they held." The slaughter of such faithful saints during the great tribulation will be massive and universal. The souls of martyred saints will be received in heaven and ushered into the immediate presence of God. The great multitude of saved people during the great tribulation comprises people from "all nations, and kindreds, and people, and tongues … who came out of the great tribulation and have washed their robes and made them white in the Blood of the Lamb (Please, read Revelation 7:9-17).

This multitude will come out of the great tribulation and pass through the gate of martyrdom into heaven.

"They loved not their lives unto death." They refused to compromise their faith in Christ and remained faithful unto death.

Consequently, they were arrayed in white robes because they are delivered from the power of sin and the influence of the antichrist and have overcome. They will stand before God and cry with a loud voice saying, "Salvation to our God which sitteth upon the throne, and unto the Lamb!" They will abide in the presence of the Lord and serve Him continually without any interruption.

XII

Chapter 12

THE SEALED 144,000 JEWS DURING
THE GREAT TRIBULATION

"And after these things I saw four angels standing on the four corners of the earth, holding the four winds of the earth, that the wind should not blow on the earth, nor on the sea, nor on any tree. And I saw another angel ascending from the east, having the seal of the living God: and he cried with a loud voice to the four angels, to whom it was given to hurt the earth and the sea, saying, Hurt not the earth, neither the sea, nor the trees, till we have sealed the servants of our God in their foreheads. And I heard the number of them which were sealed: and there were sealed an hundred and forty and four thousand of all the tribes of the children of Israel. Of the tribe of Juda were sealed twelve thousand. Of the tribe of Reuben were sealed twelve thousand. Of the tribe of Gad were sealed twelve thousand. Of the tribe of Aser were sealed twelve thousand. Of the tribe of Nephthalim were sealed twelve thousand. Of the tribe of Manasses were sealed twelve thousand. Of the tribe of Simeon were sealed twelve thousand. Of the tribe of Levi were sealed twelve thousand. Of the tribe of Issachar were sealed twelve thousand. Of the tribe of Zabulon were sealed twelve thousand. Of the tribe of Joseph were sealed twelve thousand. Of the tribe of Benjamin were sealed twelve thousand" (Revelation 7:1-8).

John the divine and the revelatory saw in a vision after the six seals that the wind of fury and judgment of God will be delayed until those numbers of God's people are sealed in their foreheads. Four angels are to hold back the winds that blow from the four points of the compass – from the north, south, east and west. Meanwhile, there will be a brief period of universal calm between the opening of the sixth seal and the seventh seal and there will be restraining of winds. During this period of holding back the winds, a specific number of God's peculiar people of the tribes of Israel would have been sealed for protection. A seal represents a stamp, a symbol or a device that bears the name of the owner, which could be stamped on someone or something bearing the name of the rightful owner or master on the forehead.

This seal on each of the 144,000 Jewish servants (12,000 from each of the 12 tribes) of God would be easily seen or prominently engraved on their foreheads as an emblem of divine ownership and a pledge of safety. The seal (mark) would be a proper designation of the fact that they are true servants of the Most-High God. These sealed servants of God would be saved after the rapture of the church and become servants of God during the great tribulation period. They will be "the first fruits to God and to the Lamb," that is, the first fruits to be redeemed from Israel. Other repentant Israelites will be saved during the great tribulation, but these sealed 144,000 Jews will be the first set to be saved.

"And I looked, and, lo, a Lamb stood on the mount Sion, and with him a hundred forty and four thousand, having his Father's name written in their foreheads…

these are they which were not defiled with women; for they are virgins. These are they which follow the Lamb whithersoever he goeth. These were redeemed from among men, being the first fruits unto God and to the Lamb" (Revelation 14:1, 4). Significantly, the tribe of Judah was named first instead of the tribe of Reuben because Reuben's birthright was taken from him "for as much as he defied his father's bed" (Genesis 49:3-4; 1 Chronicle 5:1-2).

The tribes of Dan and Ephraim are not mentioned, the tribes of Levi and Joseph take their places. The tribe of Dan completely went into idol worship (Judges 18:30). Likewise, Ephraim was addicted to idols and became an ally to the enemies of the children of Israel (Hosea 4:17). However, the remnants of Israel shall be saved before the Millennial Kingdom of Christ (Romans 9:27-28).

In Revelation 14:1-5, the 144,000 Jewish saints will face the greatest danger and still stand true, faithful, uncompromising and triumphant. The Lord will stand in the position of authority, power, glory and triumph as the reigning King and the sovereign Lord, "the Lamb stood on the mount Zion."

This is the seat of all authority, the pinnacle of glory and the dwelling place of God. "And with Him, a hundred forty and four thousand" that are redeemed, saved, purified, sanctified, set apart for God during the great tribulation, will stand with the Lamb on mount Zion "having his Father's name written in their foreheads."

This is the name of God stamped on their foreheads, it's a seal of divine ownership. "...they sang as it were a new song before the throne... and no man could learn that song but the 144,000 which were redeemed from the earth." They were counted worthy in God's presence because they keep themselves from all impurities.

Chapter 13

RESURRECTION OF THE DEAD

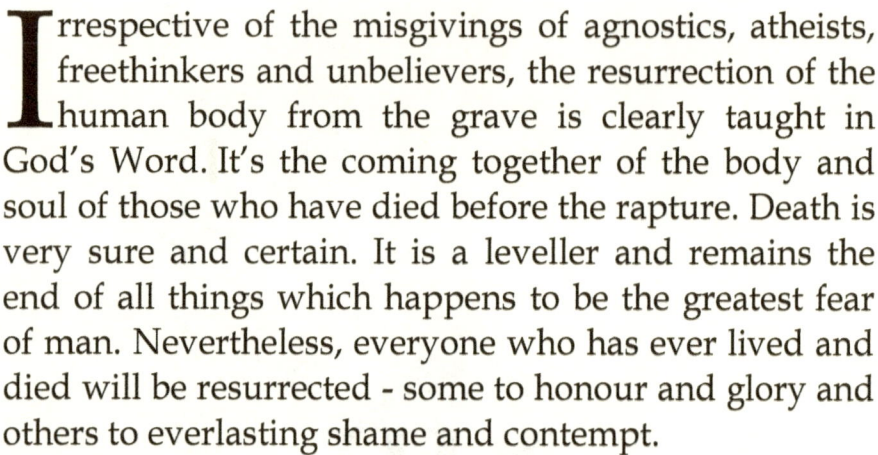

I rrespective of the misgivings of agnostics, atheists, freethinkers and unbelievers, the resurrection of the human body from the grave is clearly taught in God's Word. It's the coming together of the body and soul of those who have died before the rapture. Death is very sure and certain. It is a leveller and remains the end of all things which happens to be the greatest fear of man. Nevertheless, everyone who has ever lived and died will be resurrected - some to honour and glory and others to everlasting shame and contempt.

"Verily, verily, I say unto you, The hour is coming, and now is, when the dead shall hear the voice of the Son of God: and they that hear shall live...And many of them that sleep in the dust of the earth shall awake, some to everlasting life, and some to shame and everlasting contempt...And have hope toward God, which they themselves also allow, that there shall be a resurrection of the dead, both of the just and unjust... Marvel not at this: for the hour is coming, in the which all that are in the graves shall hear his voice, And shall come forth; they that have done good, unto the resurrection of life; and they that have done evil, unto the resurrection of damnation" (John 5:25; Daniel 12:2; Acts 24:15; John 5:28-29).

Our Lord Jesus Christ exemplified the resurrection when He arose from the dead and He's the pioneer and the stage setter for the glorious experience of resurrection. All resurrected bodies will be immortal like those of angels (Mark 12:25).

Unfortunately, many people amass wealth and live as if life shall continue on this present earth forever. When death takes our loved ones away suddenly, we run emotion during that time, pondering about it momentarily and then continue to live as if it's a strange thing that can never happen to us. Only a few people are prepared for this suddenness that sends people to their endless eternity.

To God be the glory for making it possible that the resurrection of our Lord Jesus Christ is not a fable written by any author, but a reality that happened in the real life. It is vital and fundamental to the gospel of our salvation with "many infallible proofs." However, many people are yet to believe in the final resurrection of all human beings irrespective of how they died. According to the Scriptures, there's life after death. If Jesus tarries, the human body will die, but the soul and spirit will continue to live. The souls of the saints rejoice in God's presence at death. "Then shall the dust return to the earth as it was: and the spirit shall return unto God who gave it" (Ecclesiastes 12:7).

When a sinner dies, his soul goes to hell immediately. In hell fire, sinners are conscious as they can feel, see and hear as well. All resurrection bodies will be immortal, the consciousness of true believers who die is realised in the presence of our Lord Jesus Christ. Therefore, true believers have the hope of resurrection. "And if Christ is not raised, your faith is vain; ye are yet in your sins. Then they also which are fallen asleep in Christ perished. If in this life only we have hope in Christ, we are of all men most miserable. But now is Christ risen from the dead and become the firstfruits of them that slept. For since by man came death, by man came also the resurrection of the dead" (1 Corinthians 15:17-21).

Jesus Christ our Lord is the first fruit of the dead Who rose from the grave. This is the evidence that true believers will also experience the resurrection someday. This hope of resurrection should be every believer's ultimate reason for continuous service to the Lord and for fighting the good fight of faith. The timing of the first resurrection of the just to life and the resurrection of the unjust to judgement are well-described in the Scriptures in accordance with the ordained program of God.

There's the first resurrection: "And I saw thrones, and they sat upon them, and judgment was given unto them: and I saw the souls of them that were beheaded for the witness of Jesus, and for the word of God, and which had not worshipped the beast, neither his image, neither had received his mark upon their foreheads or in their hands; and they lived and reigned with Christ a thousand years. But the rest of the dead lived not again until the thousand years were finished. This is the first resurrection. Blessed and holy is he that hath part in the first resurrection: on such the second death hath no power, but they shall be priests of God and of Christ and shall reign with him a thousand years" (Revelation 20:4-6).

The resurrection of the human body from death and the grave is the hope of our Christian faith. The first resurrection has four stages: The resurrection of Christ, the first fruit (1 Corinthians 15:3-4, 12, 20, 23). The resurrection of the true followers Christ called the church age saints at the time of rapture (1 Thessalonians 4:13-16). The resurrection of the martyrs at the end of the tribulation (Revelation 20:3-5). The resurrection of the Old Testament saints at the second advent of Christ to the earth (Daniel 12:2; Isaiah 26:19).

Moreover, the resurrection of the saints of God is variously explained in the Scriptures as the resurrection of life, the resurrection of the just, a better resurrection and the first resurrection. All saints of God that ever died would resurrect in the first resurrection. Not a soul will be left behind.

There's a second resurrection. The second resurrection is part of God's program that deals with the unsaved dead. There is a difference in time of one thousand years between the first and second resurrection (Revelation 20:5-15). The second resurrection is also called the resurrection unto damnation (John 5:29). There will be everlasting punishment and torment in the lake of fire for all who partake in the second resurrection who have missed the first resurrection (Daniel 12:2). In the intervening period between death and the resurrection, the soul of the believer goes to Paradise.

An example of this can be found in Luke 23:39-43. Where Jesus said, "…unto him, Verily I say unto thee, today shalt thou be with me in paradise." This revealed that it is from Paradise that Christ rose from the dead and ascended into Heaven. After death, the righteous have always gone to paradise and the wicked have always gone to hell. "He that hath an ear, let him hear what the Spirit saith unto the churches; To him that overcometh will I give to eat of the tree of life, which is in the midst of the paradise of God" (Revelation 2:7). Paradise is used here as a synonym for Heaven (Luke 23:43; 2 Corinthians 12:3).

Again, both paradise and hell are "temporary places of abode." As doubt and unbelief couldn't prevent the resurrection of our Lord Jesus Christ, so also the unsaved will not be able to hinder the complete resurrection program of God for both the saved and unsaved souls of men.

In the first resurrection, true believers who died in Christ will stand before the Judgment Seat of Christ to receive rewards based on laudable services to the Master Jesus and will end up in life eternal.

On the other hand, **in the second resurrection**, the sinners who will stand before the Great White Throne Judgment of God will be sent to eternal damnation. That is, these are the only two destinies for human souls; one is to be with the Lord forever and the other is to be forever separated from God's presence in the Lake of Fire! May the latter not be your portion in Jesus' name.

XIV

Chapter 14

THE SECOND COMING OF JESUS CHRIST

"Behold, he cometh with clouds; and every eye shall see him, and they also which pierced him: and all kindreds of the earth shall wail because of him. Even so, Amen. I am Alpha and Omega, the beginning and the ending, saith the Lord, which is, and which was, and which is to come, the Almighty" (Revelation 1:7-8).

Jesus is coming again and nothing can stop Him! This is the truth of the whole thing and the hope of every true believer that God is in full control of all things and is ever faithful to bring to pass His promises and word that He exalts above His name. Jesus' return from Heaven will be personal, visible, glorious and a blessed hope for which all faithful believers should constantly watch daily with all supplications up until we see Him face to face.

In Christ's first coming, He came as a baby born in a manger and a Lamb that takes away the sins of the whole world. His earthly ministry was cut short by being humiliated, crucified, resurrected and returned to Heaven "to prepare a place" for His true followers (John 14:3) with a promise to return and bring His followers to Heaven with Him. The message of the angel in Acts 1:11 lends credence to the fact that our Lord Jesus Christ shall come back in like manner and this makes the interpretation of Jesus' personal, bodily, literal and visible return undoubtedly true that He will surely return. When Jesus came for the first time into this world and as a Lamb of God, He was humiliated.

In His second coming, Jesus will come as a Lion of the tribe of Judah. The whole world shall witness His exaltation and glory. He's coming in the clouds of glory. It is indescribable because the glory of the coming of the Lord has no equal. It's next to none in the history of the world. Little did His three disciples (Peter, James, and John) see in the holy mountain of Transfiguration. His face became radiant like the sun and His raiment became shiny, exceedingly white as snow, as described in (Mark 9:2-3; Matthew 17:2), when they beheld His glory and majesty. Yet the glory at His second coming is incomparably greater and infinitely more magnificent and majestic.

Furthermore, Jesus' coming will be visible to the entire human race. This time, the world will recognise Him. The first time He came, His glory was veiled, but at His second coming, the glory, splendor and majesty will be visible. The book of Revelation says, "Behold, He cometh," and "surely, I come quickly" (Revelation 1:7; 22:20). There are over 660 general prophecies in which 330 were about Christ. 110 prophecies were fulfilled at His first coming, 220 were still to be fulfilled at His second coming. Unfortunately, many people on earth would be deep in spiritual lethargy and indifference that would characterise the people as the case in the time of Noah's flood.

The prophecy in Isaiah 9:6 that the government would be on his shoulders is yet to be fulfilled, which means, Christ will rule on earth physically. His government will be characterised by peace. Also, in Revelation 19:11-16, He's coming with the clouds and He's coming with God's presence, power and authority. He's coming as a victorious King enveloped in clouds of glory before the people of the world. Not only His three disciples will see Him this time, but "…all the tribes of the earth will wail on account of him." As some people will be rejoicing, others will be in a state of mourning.

Many of the Jews would have repented and been saved during the period of the great tribulation. Therefore, these people that pierced Him (the children of Israel), would be waiting for the return of the Messiah. They will see Him with others from Gentile nations who have been saved through the testimony of 144,000 Jews who are sealed in the book of Revelation 7:4-8 and through the preaching of a special angel in Revelation 14:6-7. All those who have not taken the mark of the beast will see Christ when He returns and they will rejoice. Hence the fulfillment of Isaiah's prophecy, "*And it shall be said in that day, Lo, this is our God; we have waited for him, and he will save us: this is the LORD; we have waited for him, we will be glad and rejoice in his salvation*" (Isaiah 25:9).

As children of Israel mourn and wail in repentance, multitudes of many Gentile nations will mourn and wail in terror and fear of judgment. The Bible reveals that Christ's advent or return will catch most people unprepared and unforgiven because of their unbelief. The doom and inescapable judgment of the impenitent and hardened sinners will make the people wail in fear and anguish while the redeemed of the Lord are full of gladness.

In summary, the church will be comforted at the second coming of the Lord, the full restoration of Israel to her sovereignty (Isaiah 32:18; 33:20-24), the judgment of the earth (Revelation 20:11-15) and the restoration of all things as planned by God (Jeremiah 12:4, 11; Romans 8:20-23). It's very important to know the difference between the rapture and the second coming of Christ. The two events are distinct and separated by seven years. The second coming refers to Christ's second coming to earth to live as He did in the first coming and all eyes will see Him. Whereas, in rapture, Christ will not come to the earth, but stop in the air where His saints will meet Him.

It is not every eye that will see Him during the rapture. As He meets the saints in the air, He will take them to Heaven where they would remain throughout the period of the great tribulation on earth. It's during this seven-year period that the marriage supper of the lamb and judgment of saints for rewards would take place in heaven. "For we must all appear before the judgment seat of Christ; that everyone may receive the things done in his body, according to that he hath done, whether it be good or bad" (2 Corinthians 5:10).

It's instructive for all true followers of Christ to watch in all things, pray always and persevere in faith because the rapture can take place any moment without warning. The second coming of Christ cannot happen until after both the rapture and the great tribulation. As part of the signs of His coming, the events of those days of the coming of the Lord will be so terrifying, so frightening, that people will literally die of heart failure when they see some strange things happening all over the world.

There will be terrifying scene developing in the heavens as the planets and stars with the appearance of other heavenly bodies would be out of control through the whole earth. "And they shall fall by the edge of the sword and shall be led away captive into all nations: and Jerusalem shall be trodden down of the Gentiles until the times of the Gentiles be fulfilled. And there shall be signs in the sun, and in the moon, and in the stars; and upon the earth distress of nations, with perplexity; the sea and the waves roaring; Men's hearts failing them for fear, and for looking after those things which are coming on the earth: for the powers of heaven shall be shaken. And then shall they see the Son of man coming in a cloud with power and great glory" (Luke 21: 24-27).

In His second coming, Christ will reign on the earth for one thousand years with the saints. His government would be characterised by unprecedented peace, prosperity and blessings on earth (Isaiah 11:1-9). Satan, the father of lies deceit, strife, contention and confusion, would be bound for the duration of Christ's Millennial reign. "And he laid hold on the dragon, that old serpent, which is the Devil, and Satan, and bound him a thousand years, and cast him into the bottomless pit, and shut him up, and set a seal upon him, that he should deceive the nations no more, till the thousand years should be fulfilled: and after that, he must be loosed a little season" (Revelation 20:2-3).

Before then, Satan and his cohorts will do all things possible to frustrate His coming again to establish the Millennial reign, but he (Satan) will be defeated just as Herod's plan to kill Jesus at His first coming failed. The battle against the Lord Jesus Christ and His saints is called the battle of Armageddon (Revelation 19:11-21; 20:1-4).

In this end time, however, the sinners are admonished to repent of all their sinful ways and accept Jesus Christ as Lord and Saviour. Backsliders are to seek reconciliation and restoration while the church, as a bride, is called to prepare and be ready, holy, spotless, watchful, prayerful and vigorously engaged in evangelism until He comes.

Chapter 15

THE BATTLE OF ARMAGEDDON

"And the sixth angel poured out his vial upon the great river Euphrates; and the water thereof was dried up, that the way of the kings of the east might be prepared. And I saw three unclean spirits like frogs come out of the mouth of the dragon, and out of the mouth of the beast, and out of the mouth of the false prophet. For they are the spirits of devils, working miracles, which go forth unto the kings of the earth and of the whole world, to gather them to the battle of that great day of God Almighty. Behold, I come as a thief. Blessed is he that watcheth, and keepeth his garments, lest he walk naked, and they see his shame. And he gathered them together into a place called in the Hebrew tongue Armageddon" (Revelation 16:12-16; Please, read Revelation 19:11-21).

As a matter of fact, the word "Armageddon" is derived from two Hebrew words that mean Mountain of Megiddo. Megiddo was a town that belonged to Manasseh at that time within the limits of Issachar (Joshua 17:11). After it was conquered and destroyed, it was later rebuilt and fortified by king Solomon (1 Kings 9:15). It was at Megiddo that Deborah and Barak defeated Sisera and his host (Judges 5:19); and it was in a battle near this that Josiah was slain by Pharaoh-Necho (2 Chronicles 35:20-25).

There was such great mourning for the death of Josiah and any other grievous mourning was likened to the mourning of Megiddo (Zechariah 12:11). Megiddo is the older Hebrew form of Armageddon, the hills of battles. Due to its strategic location, the place of Armageddon has been the site of many battles in the past. There is going to be a decisive battle as the period of great tribulation gets close to the end. It is the great battle of Armageddon because "At the end moment of the second coming of our Lord, "all nations" shall be gathered against Jerusalem to battle.

Despite the physical suffering and trauma of that time, unrepentant men will be influenced by evil spirits from Satan. The Antichrist and false prophet will gather in the battle against the Lord. No matter the strategy of the devil and his cohorts, Jesus Christ our Lord will return and set up His glorious Kingdom on earth. The book of Revelation 16 revealed that God will supernaturally dry up the river Euphrates to make way for the eastern confederacy to reach Philistine.

It is to prepare the way for the eastern army to get to Armageddon. "Three unclean spirits," demons, from the dragon (Satan), the beast (Antichrist) and the false prophet (the antichrist's associate) will produce deceptive miracles to convince "the kings of the earth and the whole world" together in battle against the Almighty God. Lying wonders and deceptive miracles done by false prophets always instigate people to oppose the true gospel and fight against the God of truth and the truth of God. At the end of the great tribulation, the impact of the supernatural acts of evil power will be so great to induce the kings to make the journey to Palestine for the final battle with the Lord. However, God will rain down from heaven His vengeful wrath of plagues on them and their followers.

"And I saw heaven opened and behold a white horse, and he that sat upon him was called Faithful and True, and in righteousness, he doth judge and make war. His eyes were as a flame of fire, and on his head were many crowns, and he had a name written, that no man knew, but he himself. And he was clothed with a vesture dipped in blood: and his name is called The Word of God. And the armies which were in heaven followed him upon white horses, clothed in fine linen, white and clean. And out of his mouth goeth a sharp sword, that with it he should smite the nations: and he shall rule them with a rod of iron: and he treadeth the winepress of the fierceness and wrath of Almighty God. And he hath on his vesture and on his thigh a name is written, KING OF KINGS, AND LORD OF LORDS" (Revelation 19:11-16).

As the Lord God poured out the 7th bowl, it will be a bowl of consummation that will bring the completion to the judgment of God upon sinful men, their injustice and their wickedness. The first three bowls bring sores, seas of blood and rivers of blood while God's justice comes as bowls and rains judgment with the scorching of sunlight, darkness upon the earth and drying of the water of Euphrates to clear the way for invading Jerusalem.

The last bowl, which is the 7th judgment of God that will bring terrible earthquakes will cause the city of Jerusalem to be divided into three parts. Cities will be destroyed and nations, mountains and islands will be displaced; and suddenly, Babylon will be remembered for judgment as well!

Great hailstones will be released out of heaven and will fall upon the inhabitants of the earth. These hail stones will weigh a talent each (about 100 pounds). With this tragedy raining down upon men, the people will continue to commit sin and will not acknowledge the sovereign God, but will keep blaspheming His holy name.

Jesus Christ will defeat all the armies of the antichrist and false prophet; they shall be cast into the lake of fire. This judgment symbolises the evil political system in the world that comes into power after the rapture of the saints, which will be judged by being given the cup of the wine of the fierce indignation of God's wrath.

XVI

Chapter 16

JUDGEMENT AND DESTRUCTION OF
END TIME BABYLON

"...I will shew unto thee the judgment of the great whore that sitteth upon many waters: With whom the kings of the earth have committed fornication, and the inhabitants of the earth have been made drunk with the wine of her fornication. So he carried me away in the spirit into the wilderness: and I saw a woman sit upon a scarlet coloured beast, full of names of blasphemy, having seven heads and ten horns. And the woman was arrayed in purple and scarlet colour, and decked with gold and precious stones and pearls, having a golden cup in her hand full of abominations and filthiness of her fornication: And upon her forehead was a name written, MYSTERY, BABYLON THE GREAT, THE MOTHER OF HARLOTS AND ABOMINATIONS OF THE EARTH. And I saw the woman drunken with the blood of the saints, and with the blood of the martyrs of Jesus: and when I saw her, I wondered with great admiration" (Revelation 17:1b-6).

Babylon is a metaphorical name for the present world and its evil system. It's not only a city or nation. It also characterises a harlot religious system as well as a political and economic system that appeared great, beautiful, wealthy and luxurious, but her appearance can be hypocritical.

It implies power, authority, wealth influence and evil which has influenced the whole world and even many church traditions throughout the centuries with strong economic power and political systems. It is a worldwide system of government, trade, entertainment and spiritual entity. The harlot religious system will commit adultery with the kings of the earth. With inscription on her forehead, "Babylon the great, mother of harlots and abominations of the earth." Ancient Babylon (the city) has already been destroyed and it is never to be rebuilt and inhabited (Jeremiah 50:1-3; Isaiah 13:17-22).

Babylon the great represents all false systems of religion dating back to Babel or Babylon (Genesis 10:8-10). The religion of Babylon originated from a man called Nimrod and his wife Semiramis. He founded Babel and the kingdom of Babylon. His wife became the first high priestess of idolatry. When Semiramis gave birth to a son, she said she was conceived miraculously by a sunbeam. The son was named Tammuz and offered as the promised deliverer of the earth.

According to legend, when Tammuz became a man, a wild bear slew him, but after 40 days of his mother's weeping, he was raised from the dead. It was in this story of Semiramis and Tammuz that the cultic worship of the mother and son began to spread throughout all the earth. The forty days of lent began, memorialising the forty days of weeping over the death of Tammuz. When the mother-son cult finally got to Rome, the

Roman Emperor Pontifex Maximus became the high priest.

Eventually, when Constantine made Christianity the state religion, all the pagan practices originating from Babylon were brought into the nominal, apostate church. The religion of mother-child worship is an abomination in the sight of God. "He said also unto me, Turn thee yet again, and thou shalt see greater abominations that they do. Then he brought me to the door of the gate of the LORD's house which was toward the north; and behold, there sat women weeping for Tammuz" (Ezekiel 8:13-14).

With Revelation 17, she is a mother of harlots and an abomination of the earth. The great harlot represents a prostitute, an unfaithful, sensual woman selling herself for money and also represents the apostate church of the last days which will be influential during the great tribulation. By holding a golden cup in her hand full of abominations and filthiness of her fornication, it revealed the inner life and secret acts of leaders and members in the apostate church with all sorts of abominations and all forms of uncleanness.

In addition, the church that has fallen and departed from the faith is portrayed as a prostitute who has piled her trade successfully and become extremely wealthy. In conjunction, the scarlet-colored beast represents luxury, splendor, royalty and influence that will support and use the false religious system to bring about world unity. At last, he will openly bear names and titles of blasphemy.

More predictions of this Babylon and the future city in Revelation chapter 18 are described as Babylon the great. It's the final commercial center of the world, the antichrist's capital. It is referred to as Babylon just as Jerusalem is called Sodom in Revelation 11:8, "And their dead bodies shall lie in the street of the great city, which spiritually is called Sodom and Egypt, where also our Lord was crucified."

The Babylon of the future will be an enormous city, a populous den of iniquity. Its destruction will be at the time of the seventh vial of judgment, close to the great tribulation. "And he cried mightily with a strong voice, saying, Babylon the great is fallen, is fallen, and is become the habitation of devils, and the hold of every foul spirit, and a cage of every unclean and hateful bird. For all nations have drunk of the wine of the wrath of her fornication, and the kings of the earth have committed fornication with her, and the merchants of the earth are waxed rich through the abundance of her delicacies" (Revelation 18:2-3).

This announcement is emphatic and irreversible. Evil spirits, demons and all kinds of unclean spirits will resort to abiding thereafter in its fall. She has beguiled and corrupted the nations of the earth, leading them into pollution, perversion and perdition, God found her guilty of many crimes and judgment has been determined on her. She joined herself to idol worship and turned to be an enemy of God's people, persecuting and fighting them. This great city of the world in the end time is going to be destroyed by God Himself. God will pour out the cup of His indignation upon Babylon.

There is mystery Babylon and materialistic Babylon. The mystery of Babylon will be destroyed by the ten kings. "And the ten horns which thou sawest upon the beast, these shall hate the whore, and shall make her desolate and naked, and shall eat her flesh, and burn her with fire" (Revelation 17:16). Whereas the destruction of materialistic Babylon will be lamented by the "... kings of the earth, who have committed fornication and lived deliciously with her, (they) shall bewail her, and lament for her, when they shall see the smoke of her burning, standing afar off for the fear of her torment, saying, Alas, alas that great city Babylon, that mighty city! for in one hour is thy judgment come" (Revelation 18:9-10).

The book of Revelation chapter 17 mentioned a woman, while Revelation chapter 18 speaks of the city. Nevertheless, the good Lord continues to warn His people not to drink the wine of the fornication of Babylon. "And I heard another voice from heaven, saying, Come out of her, my people, that ye be not partakers of her sins, and that ye receive not of her plagues" (Revelation 18:4).

Babylon always corrupts and contaminates. The universal message from God is that those who would remain watchful and holy must separate themselves from all associations of evil. "And that ye receive not of her plagues." The looming judgment of God that will come upon the guilty city will make no discrimination among those who will be found there. Therefore, escape for your life today! "Therefore, shall her plagues come in one day, death, and mourning, and famine; and she shall be utterly burned with fire: for strong is the Lord God who judgeth her" (Revelation 18:8).

There will be great mourning by the political leaders and governments of the world when the capital and the city of antichrist is destroyed. Nations and races whose power will depend entirely upon the antichrist and his capital will mourn greatly. Their economies will be greatly affected. The whole world will undergo disaster at this time and many of the great cities of the world will be destroyed and reduced to ashes. They will fall and be destroyed with Babylon. There will be great mourning and lamentation. (Please, read Revelation 18:9, 11, 15, 19).

Again, the sudden fall and destruction of Babylon will cause great mourning, weeping, wailing and lamentation. Kings and merchants of the earth who have had Babylon as their source of power, wealth, pleasure and luxury will be sorrowful "when they shall see the smoke of her burning" (Revelation 18:21). The destruction of Babylon will be violent, swift and total. It is pictured by the mighty angel throwing a huge stone into the sea. The city would be as utterly destroyed as the stone was covered by the sea.

The destruction will be so total, complete and final that the city will be no more (Verse 24). Mystery Babylon and materialistic Babylon are murderously united. The apostate church of the last days which will be supporting the antichrist and political system of the antichrist with Babylon as its capital will persecute and kill many prophets and saints who believe and follow the Lamb during the great tribulation. When the full and final judgment of the wicked, depraved, murderous Babylon eventually comes, Heaven will celebrate the victory and rejoice at last.

XVII

Chapter 17

MILLENNIAL REIGN OF CHRIST

"And he laid hold on the dragon, that old serpent, which is the Devil, and Satan, and bound him a thousand years, and cast him into the bottomless pit, and shut him up, and set a seal upon him, that he should deceive the nations no more, till the thousand years should be fulfilled: and after that he must be loosed a little season. and I saw thrones, and they sat upon them, and judgment was given unto them: and I saw the souls of them that were beheaded for the witness of Jesus, and for the word of God, and which had not worshipped the beast, neither his image, neither had received his mark upon their foreheads, or in their hands; and they lived and reigned with Christ a thousand years. But the rest of the dead lived not again until the thousand years were finished. This is the first resurrection. Blessed and holy is he that hath part in the first resurrection: on such the second death hath no power, but they shall be priests of God and of Christ and shall reign with him a thousand years. And when the thousand years are expired, Satan shall be loosed out of his prison" (Revelation 20:2-7).

Millennium is a term is derived from the Latin word Mille, which means thousand. Therefore, the one-thousand-year reign of our Lord Jesus Christ on earth is referred to as Christ's Millennial Reign of the full manifestation of His glory and commencement of the seventh dispensation (the system of order of God's government on earth). Before we proceed in this subject, we should briefly consider the different dispensations:

The Dispensation of Innocence – Adam and Eve were created perfectly in the image of God with an eternal soul, free will and the ability to procreate. With all these qualities, however, man disobeyed God, bringing sin, curse and death into the world. This is the shortest dispensation from the creation to the fall of man (Genesis 1:1-3; 28-30; 2:15-17). That is, from man's expulsion from the Garden of Eden until the Flood was 1,656 years.

The Dispensation of Conscience – Men were left to rule themselves by their own will and conscience. Man was not created like a robot, but as an image of God, he possesses the ability to make the right choice. Therefore, God's expectation from man during this time was to learn and discover that conscience, being poor, could not guide him without the help of God, the Creator. In that dispensation, only Abel, Enoch and Noah were found upright to the point that "… God saw that the wickedness of man was great in the earth and that every imagination of the thoughts of his heart was only evil continually. And it repented the LORD that he had made man on the earth, and it grieved him at his heart" (Genesis 6:5-6).

God, in His patience and being a righteous Judge, couldn't continue to condone sin forever, always deals with the problem of sin. "And the LORD said, I will destroy man whom I have created from the face of the earth; both man, and beast, and the creeping thing, and the fowls of the air; for it repenteth me that I have made them. But Noah found grace in the eyes of the LORD" (Genesis 6:7-8). Only eight people, including Noah, were saved and brought forth into a new dispensation.

The Dispensation of Human Government – Theologians made it clear that from the Flood to the confusion of tongues at Babel and scattering was about 429 years (In between Genesis 8:20 and Genesis 11:9). God confused the language of men and scattered them abroad to create different nations, cultures and settlements. Noah, his wife, his three sons and their wives began to repopulate the earth. "And the sons of Noah, that went forth of the ark, were Shem, and Ham, and Japheth: and Ham is the father of Canaan. These are the three sons of Noah: and of them was the whole earth overspread" (Genesis 9:18-19).

God allowed the civil government to be appointed to protect man from his own sinful nature. This means that man is still responsible to use this authority to enforce righteousness to protect the sanctity of human life. Shem was the father of the Mediterranean region dwellers and eventually the Jews (Shem is Semitic in Latin). Ham's descendants spread into the African continent while Japheth's children migrated into Eurasia (Europe and Asia).

The Dispensation of Promise – This dispensation spans from the call of Abraham to the giving of the Mosaic Law at Mount Sinai, it's about 430 years. "Now the LORD had said unto Abram, Get thee out of thy country, and from thy kindred, and from thy father's house, unto a land that I will shew thee: And I will make of thee a great nation, and I will bless thee, and make thy name great; and thou shalt be a blessing: And I will bless them that bless thee, and curse him that curseth thee: and in thee shall all families of the earth be blessed" (Genesis 12:1-3).

God called Abram and changed his name to Abraham with a promise that he would be the father of a multitude of nations. It is the dispensation of "Promise" because the God of the covenant made a promise with Abraham and his descendants who lived in the Promised Land to the giving of the Mosaic Law at Mount Sinai.

The Dispensation of Law – This dispensation lasted approximately 1,526 years and covered all aspects of the Scripture from Exodus 19:4-5 to John 19:30. "Ye have seen what I did unto the Egyptians, and how I bare you on eagles' wings and brought you unto myself. Now therefore, if ye will obey my voice indeed, and keep my covenant, then ye shall be a peculiar treasure unto me above all people: for all the earth is mine... When Jesus, therefore, had received the vinegar, he said, it is finished: and he bowed his head, and gave up the ghost." This dispensation ranges from Mt. Sinai until Christ Jesus fulfilled the Law with His death on Mount of Calvary.

The Dispensation of Grace/Church Age – This dispensation is called the "age of grace" or "Church age." It occurs between the 69th and 70th weeks of Daniel's prophecy (Daniel 9:24). "And I say also unto thee, that thou art Peter, and upon this rock, I will build my church; and the gates of hell shall not prevail against it" (Matthew 16:18). Grace is God's benevolence to the underserving people in the world because of sins. This grace of God brings justification (salvation from sins) by faith in Christ Jesus, sanctification (purification from inward depravity) by the blood of Christ and the Holy Ghost baptism. These three are definite Christian experiences for true followers of Christ. "Being justified freely by his grace through the redemption that is in Christ Jesus: Whom God hath set forth to be a propitiation through faith in his blood, to declare his righteousness for the remission of sins that are past, through the forbearance of God" (Romans 3:24-25).

The Dispensation of Christ's Millennial Reign – This represents the Kingdom of Christ (1,000-year reign) on earth. *"Blessed and holy is he that hath part in the first resurrection: on such the second death hath no power, but* *they shall be priests of God and of Christ and shall reign with him a thousand years"* (Revelation 20:6).

Millennium is the seventh dispensation that follows the Battle of Armageddon and the destruction of God's enemies (Revelation 19:11-21). It is the dispensation when Christ will rule in power and authority over everything on earth. It's a period that will be characterised by remarkable peace, uncommon prosperity, uninterrupted righteousness, unexampled preservation, outstanding purity, unending joy, resounding divine health as well as Eden-like restoration of all things on earth. It will be a utopia in reality!

The Millennium will be a replica or prototype of Eden where the ferocity of wild animals disappears because of the restoration to their pristine nature. Isaiah 11 captures it graphically; verses 6-10 reads, "The wolf also shall dwell with the lamb, and the leopard shall lie down with the kid; and the calf and the young lion and the fatling together; and a little child shall lead them. And the cow and the bear shall feed; their young ones shall lie down together: and the lion shall eat straw like the ox. And the sucking child shall play on the hole of the asp, and the weaned child shall put his hand on the cockatrice' den. They shall not hurt nor destroy in all my holy mountain: for the earth shall be full of the knowledge of the LORD, as the waters cover the sea.

And in that day there shall be a root of Jesse, which shall stand for an ensign of the people; to it shall the Gentiles seek: and his rest shall be glorious."

The extraordinary lifespan of natural people during the Millennium will be like the people during the Great Deluge or the Flood. Isaiah 65:20 puts it aptly: "There shall be no more thence an infant of days, nor an old man that hath not filled his days: for the child shall die an hundred years old; but the sinner being an hundred years old shall be accursed." Jesus Christ will rule the nations with a rod of iron; then every knee will bow, and every tongue shall confess that Jesus Christ is Lord to the glory of God the Father. Hallelujah! The Kingdom of God will be fully regulated by His righteousness and spiritual laws.

Prior to this glorious reign of Christ, the Church would have gone and ascended at the rapture to pave way for the commencement of the last week of Daniel's prophecy, the seven years of great tribulation and the reign of the antichrist that will end with the second coming of Christ with the church to establish the government of righteousness on earth. "And Enoch also, the seventh from Adam, prophesied of these, saying, Behold, the Lord cometh with ten thousand of his saints" (Jude 1:14. Please, read 1 Thessalonians 4:1-18; Matthew 24:21-22).

The government of this world, under the control of Satan, will resist the coming of Christ, but Satan will fail. The Lord Jesus will overcome him and his cohorts at the Battle of Armageddon. The Beast and the false prophet will be cast alive into a lake of fire burning with brimstone. And Satan, the dragon that is fierce and wicked, "the old serpent" that is subtle and cunning, the archenemy behind the fall of man in the garden of the Eden, "the Devil" – the accuser of the brethren, "Satan" – the adversary that ruled and ruined this present world, will be arrested by the angel of God that came down from Heaven, "having the key of the bottomless pit and a great chain in his hand." Satan will be chained and imprisoned in the bottomless pit for one thousand years (Revelation 20:1-3) by the angel with the superior mighty power of God.

As soon as the devil was bounded cast into the bottomless pit, John "… saw thrones, and they sat upon them, and judgement was given unto them" (Revelation 20:4). It's important to know that these thrones are the privilege and promised seats that triumphant saints would sit upon to pronounce judgement upon the people that rejected God's grace and mercy.

On Christ's first advent on earth, He brought grace; at His second coming, He will execute justice. He will be the benevolent Dictator ruling the whole world through the process called a theocracy (the rule of God). The resurrected saints of all times will participate in the management of Christ's government during the Millennial reign on earth. At the end of the Millennial reign, Satan will be released and permitted to operate all over the world for a while (Revelation 20:3).

Satan again, "shall go out to deceive the nations which are in four quarters of the earth" and execute the wicked passions of mankind to fight against the government of Christ on earth to overthrow it. Through his revolt and subtlety, multitudes will be deceived. With all the rebellion against God, a dreadful army of Satan laid siege against Christ and His saints and Jerusalem. They shall be consumed by fire from Heaven (Revelation 20:9). After this defeat comes the final tribulation and judgement of God on the devil, his antichrist and the false prophet.

XVIII

Chapter 18

THE BATTLE OF GOG AND MAGOG

"And when the thousand years are expired, Satan shall be loosed out of his prison, and shall go out to deceive the nations which are in the four quarters of the earth, Gog, and Magog, to gather them together to battle: the number of whom is as the sand of the sea. And they went up on the breadth of the earth, and compassed the camp of the saints about, and the beloved city: and fire came down from God out of heaven and devoured them" (Revelation 20:7-9).

Magog was a grandson of Noah that settled to the far north of Israel. The book of Ezekiel 38 and 39 described them as skilled warriors. Magog the son of Japheth was mentioned in the Old Testament on four occasions (Genesis 10:2; 1 Chronicles 1:5; Ezekiel 38:2; 39:6).

Whereas Gog is described as "of the land of Magog, the prince of Rosh, Meshech, and Tubal." As these people demonstrated rebellion against God and hostility towards God's people in the Old Testament, so also are they going to repeat it in the end time. Hence, the book of Revelation uses Ezekiel's prophecy about Gog and Magog to portray a final end-time attack on the nation of Israel. The battle of Gog and Magog is the future invasion by a coalition of nations to fight God's people.

There are two significant battles immediately after the rapture of the saints. The first is right before the Second Coming (the battle of Armageddon) and the other is at the end of the Millennium (the battle of Gog and Magog). They are similar in that they will be massive battles involving great destruction that destroys the enemies of God and thereafter ushers in the original plan of God on the earth. The battle of Gog and Magog will be the final battle of God's enemies after one thousand years of the millennial reign of Christ. John the Beloved, in Revelation, had Ezekiel's perfect description of God's judgments on Gog and his allied forces in the way he described the final destruction of Satan and his cohorts.

There are similarities between Ezekiel's prediction with Revelation 20. Both armies are formidable from every quarter of the earth (Ezekiel 38:9, 15, 16). Both plan to destroy God's people (Ezekiel 38:10-12). Both are destroyed "in the latter days" (Ezekiel 38:16). Both lost in the battle and are destroyed by great hailstone, fire and brimstone (Ezekiel 38:22). In Revelation 20:8, it clearly reveals that "Gog and Magog" are the nations from the four quarters of the earth" - meaning Satan and his cohorts that will wage war against God and His people in the latter days, at the end of time.

During this time, Satan will be set loose from the bottomless pit to do his worst for the last time because he has a limited time. He's going to gather his formidable armies from the quarters of the earth to fight against Israel to conquer the land. The world's allied forces will penetrate the borders of Israel from the northern side to conquer Jerusalem (blessed city) and take over as their new seat of power as described by prophet Ezekiel. The nations will argue that war against Israel is justifiable enough, but God will never allow them to succeed (Ezekiel 38:4-6). In all these, Satan's rebellion against God's purpose will come to an end as fire will come down from heaven to devour them. Finally, the devil and his cohorts will lose this battle and end up in the lake of fire!

XIX

Chapter 19

GREAT WHITE THRONE JUDGEMENT

Great white throne judgement is the final judgement of all people from all nations and all generations who refused to come before the throne of grace while alive on earth to receive mercy and salvation through Jesus Christ – God's sacrifice for man's sin. Hence they will have no choice than to come before God's throne of judgement. *"And I saw a great white throne, and him that sat on it, from whose face the earth and the heaven fled away; and there was found no place for them. And I saw the dead, small and great, stand before God; and the books were opened: and another book was opened, which is the book of life: and the dead were judged out of those things which were written in the books, according to their works. And the sea gave up the dead which were in it; and death and hell delivered up the dead which were in them: and they were judged every man according to their works. And death and hell were cast into the lake of fire. This is the second death"* (Revelation 20:11-15).

The throne that someone sat on is the throne of the great God, the most-High God, the great Judge of the whole universe, Who is supreme; He is the highly exalted sitting on the high throne of the final judgement of the end times. Whereas the white throne is a dazzling throne, white, bright and shining - from it, spotless, flawless, faultless, irreversible justice will come forth upon men where they will all stand before God to give an account of their deeds. Many people in this world today are living in delusion as they assume that things will continue as they are forever! – hoping that no one would be held accountable for how they live their lives on earth.

Unfortunately, this is a great delusion and deception of the devil to lure many people into carelessness and eventual retribution. Judgement day is nearer than many people realise. The looming judgement of God is sure as He has prepared to pour His plagues on the offensive and unrighteous that refused to change their evil ways. The plagues of God's judgement are coming and they shall be universal so much so that no sinner can escape from them. God's purpose then will be to abolish evil once and for all when He decides to bring the world to an end. Those who lived to please God stand above the evil that would befall the rest of sinful humanity.

This final judgement of sinners (the living and the dead, small and great) is known as the great white throne judgement (Please, read John 5:22; Matthew 25:31-32). This judgment will take place after the millennial reign of Christ and after Satan and his fallen angels are thrown into the lake of fire where the beast and the false prophet are. The world is corrupt and polluted with all sorts of sins and wickedness. Man continues to rebel and disobey God's word. For a long time, it repented the Lord that He had made man on the earth, for every imagination of the thoughts of man's heart has been evil continually (Genesis 6:5-6). The reason God "... hath appointed a day in which He will judge the world in righteousness..." (Acts 17:30-31).

It will be a fearful and frightening sight as the earth and the heaven, that is, the earth elements and heaven firmaments, will flee away. What fright as sinners stand alone before the great Judge! All categories of sinners (dead and alive) from Adam to date will be judged for neglecting the call to salvation. "How shall we escape, if we neglect so great salvation, which at the first began to be spoken by the Lord and was confirmed unto us by them that heard him" (Hebrews 2:3).

All backsliders in all generations who denied the faith of Him that once bought them and all who deny the deity of Jesus Christ, the only begotten Son of God (John 3:18, 36) will be judged! These are the sceptics, the idol worshippers, the atheists and all religious hypocrites (Matthew 23:27). Every unrighteous act, feeling or imagination that was not cleansed by the blood of the Lamb will be judged on that day of the Lord. In addition, the secret deeds of men like immorality, secret bribery, drunkenness, doing hard drugs, paedophilia, bestiality, pornography, fornication, abortion among other sins, will all be judged. There's a reward in heaven for everything done under the sun "whether good or bad" (2 Corinthians 5:10b).

"Every idle word that men shall speak; they shall give account thereof in the day of judgement." Every gossip, backbiting or slander against our neighbours and fellow believers will be judged. All foolish unedifying words, corrupt, graceless words, defamatory and abusive words against others will be accounted for in the great day of judgement. "For by thy words, thou shall be condemned" (Matthew 12:37).

The final judgement will not be arbitrary and will not be determined by man's rank, position, status or profession. It will be based on the record of men's secret acts and the total influence of character. "And death and hell were cast into the lake of fire. This is the second death" (Revelation 20:14). I believe that the Lake of Fire referred to here will be hotter and more horrible than the molten magma from volcanic eruption. Magma or *molten magma* is extremely hot; it is around 700 to 1300 degrees Celsius which, ordinarily, we considered to be extremely hot for anything life can withstand.

During this time, hell and death would have been cast into the lake of fire, which means that it will be too difficult for man to die or cease from existence. Even death (regarded as the separation of soul and body) being the last enemy of man to be defeated, would have been cast into the lake of fire. It will exist no more after the final judgement of God. The reign of death in humanity will come to an end.

The righteous will live forever with God in Heaven while the unrighteous will live forever in the Lake of Fire and be everlastingly separated from God! "And whosoever was not found written in the book of life was cast into the lake of fire." In view of this, the time to seek salvation and escape from the wrath to come is now! There's no other way to escape God's judgement and punishment except to quickly retrace one's steps from all unrighteousness and rebellious acts, pleading with the Lord to obtain mercy, forgiveness and grace to shun all forms of evil and to live according to the dictates of God's word and His Holy Spirit.

Chapter 20

THE NEW HEAVEN AND THE NEW EARTH

"And I saw a new heaven and a new earth: for the first heaven and the first earth were passed away; and there was no more sea. And I John saw the holy city, new Jerusalem, coming down from God out of heaven, prepared as a bride adorned for her husband. And I heard a great voice out of heaven saying, Behold, the tabernacle of God is with men, and he will dwell with them, and they shall be his people, and God himself shall be with them, and be their God. And God shall wipe away all tears from their eyes; and there shall be no more death, neither sorrow, nor crying, neither shall there be any more pain: for the former things are passed away. And he that sat upon the throne said, Behold, I make all things new. And he said unto me, Write: for these words are true and faithful. And he said unto me, It is done. I am Alpha and Omega, the beginning and the end. I will give unto him that is athirst of the fountain of the water of life freely. He that overcometh shall inherit all things; and I will be his God, and he shall be my son. But the fearful, and unbelieving, and the abominable, and murderers, and whoremongers, and sorcerers, and idolaters, and all liars, shall have their part in the lake which burneth with fire and brimstone: which is the second death" (Revelation 21:1-8).

The New Heaven and the New Earth are sometimes referred to as the "eternal state." The holy city, new Jerusalem, coming down from God out of Heaven. The heavenly city is the eternal inheritance that God has prepared for all who love and worship Him in Spirit and in truth. That means the great, holy, eternal Heaven will have a new Jerusalem as its capital coming out of Heaven from God. This is the eternal domicile of saints from all ages. "… a city which hath foundations, whose builder and maker is God" Himself.

Jesus Christ our Lord spoke about this when He said, "And if I go and prepare a place for you, I will come again, and receive you unto myself; that where I am, there ye may be also" (John 14:3). This heavenly city is a place of happiness without sorrow, life without death, contentment without crying, pleasure without pain, fellowship without separation, gladness without sadness, satisfaction without disappointment and perpetual health without sickness or weakness. This city was prepared for you (as a true follower of Christ) by God Himself and revealed to John the Apostle.

The New Heaven and the New Earth will be the rendezvous of restoration of fellowship that humans lost in the garden of Eden because God will be with us, dwell among us and be our God. True believers are strangers and pilgrims here on earth and here, "we have no continuing city, but we (should) seek one to come" (Hebrews 13:14). Heaven is a prepared place for a prepared people. The present universe will be rolled up, removed, changed and recreated.

In the coming New Heaven and New earth, there will be no sea, no sanctuary, no sin, no sickness, no sorrow or sadness and no separation from the Most High God.

All the righteous will enjoy a perfect state and there will be perfect, perpetual intimacy with God throughout eternity! Heaven is our home; we are only God's ambassadors on earth. The appearance of the city reveals unparalleled beauty and grandeur. The size, the combination of vibrant colors and the layout of the city make it glow as a brilliant gem (a precious stone) in the city (Please, read Revelation 21:9-27).

The great, holy, eternal city is also called "the Bride" because of its virgin beauty, unstained with sin. Everything there is transparent, "clear as crystal," "like unto clear glass." The gate shall not shut at all. There will be no night there; there will be no obstruction and nothing to block the effulgent blazing of the glory of God. The beauty of the Holy City, which is the New Jerusalem, is beyond human description. It is ineffable!

About 15,000 miles, the streets are made of pure gold, as clear as glass. The entire city walls are made of jasper and the foundations are garnished with all manner of precious stones. It has twelve gates of twelve pearls. This is a city without any temple because the Lord God Almighty and the Lamb will be the temple of it. No stretch of imagination can fathom the architecture and glory of this out-of-the-world city!

'And I saw no temple therein: for the Lord God Almighty and the Lamb is the temple of it. And the city had no need of the sun, neither of the moon, to shine in it: for the glory of God did lighten it, and the Lamb is the light thereof" (Revelation 21:22-23). The pure river of the water of life, clear as crystal, proceeds out of the throne of God and of the Lamb.

The tree of life by the sides of this river bears twelve manners of fruits monthly. The fruits and leaves are for the healing of the nations (Revelation 22:2). Nothing could give a more striking view of the magnificence of the future home of the saints. "And there shall in no wise (by any means) enter into it anything that defileth."

All who live unclean lives will be excluded from the Holy City! No sinner will enter into the holy city to stain or desecrate it. All sinners will be forever banished from the presence of God and from the holy city, but the overcomers will then inherit all things! "But as it is written, Eye hath not seen, nor ear heard, neither have entered into the heart of man, the things which God hath prepared for them that love him." (1 Corinthians 2:9). Would you not rather become a citizen of this Holy City (whose Builder and Maker is God Almighty) freely by accepting Jesus Christ as your Lord and Saviour now? The choice is yours.

Chapter 21

ETERNITY IN HELL: THE LAKE OF FIRE

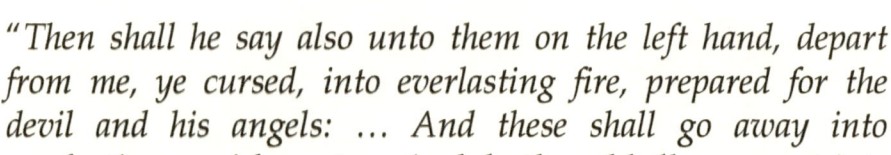

"Then shall he say also unto them on the left hand, depart from me, ye cursed, into everlasting fire, prepared for the devil and his angels: ... And these shall go away into everlasting punishment ... And death and hell were cast into the lake of fire. This is the second death" (Matthew 25:41,46a; Revelation 20:14).

Hell is the final abode where sinners of all ages shall be punished and suffer torment forever and ever because of their outright disobedience to God and rejection of the call of salvation made available through our Lord Jesus Christ. It's a place that was originally prepared for the devil and his angels, not for man who was created in God's image. Adam and Eve disobeyed the Lord God, the death sentence came upon humanity and had remained so ever since, but as a mark of God's mercy, love and goodness, He made provision for the salvation of man so that the Paradise lost can be regained through Christ.

Therefore, hell is the consequence of rejecting the call of God unto salvation. But "... Blessed are the dead which die in the Lord from henceforth: Yea, saith the Spirit, that they may rest from their labours; and their works do follow them" (Revelation 14:13). Before one could die in the Lord, he must have repented of his sinful nature and believed in the vicarious or substitutionary death on the cross of Calvary. Even before the incarnation of Christ, there were people in the Old Testament who had a glorious exit because of their saving faith in the Lord (Hebrew 11:13, 16). Many of the Old Testament believers renounced their idolatrous ways, repented of their sins and turned to the Lord in their days.

Since death is a common human experience, it's only those that died in the Lord who shall be with Him in Heaven because 'And as it is appointed unto men once to die, but after this the judgment… The wicked shall be turned into hell, and all the nations that forget God" (Hebrew 9:27; Psalms 9:17). Hence death is not the ultimate end of man because man possesses an immortal soul called spirit which animals don't have. That's why animals don't go to Heaven or Hell.

The word "Hell" is found about fifty-four times in the King James Version of the Bible - 31 in the Old Testament, and 23 in the New Testament. Its translation in Hebrew, Sheol, occurs 31 times, while the Greek interpretation "Gehena,""hades" and the Latin interpretation "Tartarus" occur 12 times, 10 times and 1 time respectively.

When a sinner dies, his soul immediately proceeds to Hell where, with full consciousness, he tastes the untold pains and suffering that Hell offers. The real story of Lazarus and the rich man told by our Lord Jesus Christ is the perfect illustration of the eternal punishment awaiting sinners. This was not some fiction, fable or parable because the characters mentioned once lived on earth. You will agree with me that Abraham is not fake or fiction, neither is Lazarus nor the rich man. Here is the account made by Jesus Hiimself: "And in hell he lifts up his eyes, being in torments, and seeth Abraham afar off, and Lazarus in his bosom. And he cried and said, Father Abraham, have mercy on me, and send Lazarus, that he may dip the tip of his finger in water, and cool my tongue; for I am tormented in this flame. But Abraham said, Son, remember that thou in thy lifetime receivedst thy good things, and likewise Lazarus evil things: but now he is comforted, and thou art tormented" (Luke 16:23-25).

Here, Christ revealed to us that Hell is a place where the memory of the lost comes alive. The rich man from the story above remembered his extravagant lifestyle while on earth as well as his five brothers yet unsaved. The truth of the whole matter is that, when we die, our spirits go to God to receive judgment, retribution, reward or punishment, depending on what we believed and what we did while on earth.

God will judge "every man according to their works." The question that you need to answer is, how, where and in what condition will you be when death comes knocking at your door? Will you die as the rich fool who had materials things of this world, but did not prepare for endless eternity? Where will you be when you die? Hell was not initially created for you as a human being because you are created in God's image, but your wrong choice would take you there by rejecting the Saviour! No one is going to Hell because of sin, but for refusing God's only offer of salvation through Jesus. Hell is a place of perpetual burning "where their worm dies not, and the fire is not quenched" (Mark 9:44).

Hell is a terrible place of conscious torments for all sinners and backsliders because of the consequence of sin which is eternal damnation! The Apocalypse harps, "The same shall drink of the wine of the wrath of God, which is poured out without mixture into the cup of his indignation; and he shall be tormented with fire and brimstone in the presence of the holy angels, and in the presence of the Lamb: And the smoke of their torment ascendeth up for ever and ever: and they have no rest day nor night, who worship the beast and his image, and whosoever receiveth the mark of his name" (Revelation 14:10-11).

If you Miss Heaven, you cannot miss Hell – the Lake of Fire! There is no neutral ground. Limbo is strange to Scriptures and so, it's a dangerous fallacy to avoid.

XXII

Chapter 22

TWO WAYS AND TWO DESTINATIONS – MAKE YOUR CHOICE!

"Enter ye in at the strait gate: for wide is the gate, and broad is the way, that leadeth to destruction, and many there be which go in thereat: Because strait is the gate, and narrow is the way, which leadeth unto life, and few there be that find it" (Matthew 7:13-14).

Every one of us lives through a journey on earth and is faced with decisions on the choice of path we are to tread. Man was not created as a robot, but to know how to make a choice in life. In other words, it is a journey from time to eternity in which we need to make a choice for ourselves. There are always two paths to choose from and each of them has its eternal consequences. The way we choose defines who we are to God - friend or enemy. The way we walk determines our destination, either in Heaven or Hell. The popular way is broad and wide. Its path is filled with fleshly pleasure, ease and wickedness. It offers all that satisfy the flesh such as fornication, adultery, selfishness, drunkenness, power, popularity to mention a few that damn the soul of man.

The truth remains that, "there is a way that seemeth right unto a man, but the end thereof are the ways of death" (Proverbs 16:25). The broad way leads to death –

eternal death, a place of everlasting punishment and regret. The wide gate is the gate through which many people enter life from the age of accountability. The pro-choice gate accommodates every load of sin and evil that people carry along without any restriction or restraint. This is the way the multitudes love most with licentious liberty for everyone desiring to go through the broadway.

The Pharisees, religious proselytes, Sadducees, the hypocrites, reprobates, deceivers, covetous, self-righteous, fleshly, pleasure-seekers, sensual, despisers of God, opposers of righteousness, public and private sinners, unashamed criminals, tempters, unconverted moralists, the proud, the worldly, violent men, the vile, wicked people, vulnerable youths and backsliders are all going through the wide gate that leads to the broad way of damnable Hell!

This broadway is a dangerous route for all travellers. It is a very dangerous way to choose because it leads multitudes to irreversible eternal damnable destruction! God is the God of mercy; it is not His will that anyone should perish, but that all should turn from their broadway of sin to the narrow, stony and rough road filled with righteousness and holiness. It leads to a place of splendour and eternal joy in Heaven where God dwells. Dear reader, make a wise choice. This is the reason God sent His only begotten Son to the world to save humanity from their broad way.

"For God so loved the world, that he gave his only begotten Son, that whosoever believeth in him should not perish, but have everlasting life... He that believeth on the Son hath everlasting life: and he that believeth not the Son shall not see life, but the wrath of God abideth on him" (John 3:16, 36). This is the way to salvation from sin and its consequences.

The way to salvation from sin is to believe in the Lord Jesus Christ. The moment you repent of your sins and believe in the Lord Jesus, even if you are the worst sinner, you are saved! You believe that He came to this world and died for your sins to save you. You believe that you are a sinner by birth and you can't save yourself. You believe that He has the power to cleanse you from sin. You get born again if you can confess your sins to Him and promise that you will never go back to them and accept Him as your Lord and personal Saviour. "But as many as received him, to them gave he power to become the sons of God, even to them that believe on his name "(John 1:12).

Salvation is entirely by grace and grace has the power to transform the vilest sinner into a saint. Jesus Christ has paid the full price for our redemption and we need to appropriate the sacrifice into our lives to be saved by grace through faith in the atoning blood of Jesus Christ shed for us on the cross of Calvary. "That if thou shalt confess with thy mouth the Lord Jesus, and shalt believe in thine heart that God hath raised him from the dead, thou shalt be saved. For with the heart, man believeth unto righteousness, and with the mouth, confession is made unto salvation" (Romans 10:9-10).

We have no righteousness or good works that merits the favour of God; rather, it is grace alone that wrought the miracle of salvation in us. Once you are saved from the power of sins, you begin a new journey of life into life eternal and you are no more walking in the broad way that lead to damnation and a place of everlasting torment. In this new way to life eternal, you have a part to play for God's grace to continue in your life.

You begin to read the word of God (Holy Bible) and obey it daily, praying daily and join the fellowship of God's people in a Bible-believing church regularly for growth and development. This is the new life of grace and when we allowed grace to grow in us, it will make our lives beautiful before all men and the Lord. It also produces in us the purity of life that pleases God. Grace enables us to overcome all ups and downs of life and keeps us true to our calling as children of God.

Self-indulgence, self-pleasing, carelessness and frivolity can make us lose the grace of God. Our God has no desire in them that draw back from this new way of life that leads to life eternal. "Now the just shall live by faith: but if any man draws back, my soul shall have no pleasure in him" (Hebrews 10:38; Please, read Hebrews John 17:17-19; 12:14).

Furthermore, God expects that, since we are forgiven our numerous sins, we should be at peace with our fellowmen. It is obvious that offences will come among the children of God due to imperfection, but the grace of God that brought salvation to us is able to help settle the differences. Forgiveness is easy when Jesus Christ has been enthroned in the heart through repentance and when there is a willingness to obey Christ's command.

Examples of those that forgave freely which Heaven took cognizance of their actions abound in the Scriptures. Joseph forgave his brothers (Genesis 45:5-15; 50:19-21). David forgave Saul (1 Samuel 24:1-22; 2 Samuel 19:1-13). Jesus forgave those that crucified Him (Luke 23:24). Stephen forgave those who stoned him to death (Acts 7:54-60). It is possible for us to say we have forgiven, but still harbour some grudges over the offences committed and this is why inner freedom becomes necessary.

There is an outward freedom as well as an inward freedom. At Salvation, the shoots and roots of sin are destroyed, but the nature of sin must be controlled by the Holy Spirit in the believer. The fruit of the Spirit, which is expected to be manifested at salvation, is deepened when the inward depravity is dealt with by walking in the Spirit. Jesus Christ our Lord prayed for the sanctification (state of holiness) of His disciples. However, believers must consciously avoid sin and please God at all times.

"Sanctify them through thy truth: thy word is truth. As thou hast sent me into the world, even so, have I also sent them into the world. And for their sakes, I sanctify myself, that they also might be sanctified through the truth" (John 17:17-19). The blood of Jesus is efficacious enough, hence the charge to every believer to live victoriously over sin by the lesson of grace which states:

"For the grace of God that bringeth salvation hath appeared to all men, Teaching us that, denying ungodliness and worldly lusts, we should live soberly, righteously, and godly, in this present world; Looking for that blessed hope, and the glorious appearing of the great God and our Saviour Jesus Christ; Who gave himself for us, that he might redeem us from all iniquity, and purify unto himself a peculiar people, zealous of good works" (Titus 2:11-14). The disciples were born again - following Jesus, but we could see the evidence of position seeking, bigotry, inconsiderate action and indignation in them (Mark 9:33-35; Luke 9:51-56). Hence, there was a need for freedom from moral corruption if they were to be set apart for sacred use.

Likewise, Paul the apostle, in his prayer to the church in Thessalonica said, "And the very God of peace sanctify you wholly; and I pray God your whole spirit and soul and body be preserved blameless unto the coming of our Lord Jesus Christ. Faithful is he that calleth you, who also will do it" (1Thesalonians 5:23-24). How can the soul, spirit and body be preserved blameless unto the coming of our Lord Jesus Christ? We must see the need for activating our inward freedom from the depraved nature daily. This is not the product of self-struggle, but that of entirely surrendering ourselves to the Lord. It is grace alone that can accomplish purity in any willing heart. This is possible because God is in the business and has made provision for our sanctification or purity of heart in Christ Jesus.

After the believer sanctifies or sets himself apart from distractions of carnality, God offers him the fullness of His power to do exploits. "And, behold, I send the promise of my Father upon you: but tarry ye in the city of Jerusalem, until ye be endued with power from on high…But ye shall receive power, after that the Holy Ghost comes upon you: and ye shall be witnesses unto me both in Jerusalem, and in all Judaea, and in Samaria, and unto the uttermost part of the earth" (Luke 24:49; Acts 1:8).

For every believer who sincerely desires the gifts that come with Holy Spirit baptism at salvation, the numerous promises of God's willingness to give and His provision for this experience give a solid basis for earnestly seeking for more of God. Moreover, the Scripture cannot be broken. The mighty outpouring of the Holy Spirit is promised to "all flesh" (Joel 2:28-29). Everyone who meets God's condition can receive God's abundance of the promised Spirit. The initial and physical evidence of Holy Spirit baptism is either the speaking in tongues or any other gift manifestation as the Holy Spirit distributes to each believer. However, receiving the Holy Spirit is more than just speaking in tongues. The power of God that accompanies that experience equips the believers to do great exploits for the Lord in this end time up until the Lord comes.

The power of God counsels, comforts, helps, guides, illuminates, inspires and reveals the deep things of God to every believer that chooses this narrow way that leads to eternal life. Summarily, at salvation, we start a new journey of life with Christ Jesus - a new way that leads to eternal life. "Jesus saith unto him, I am the way, the truth, and the life: no man cometh unto the Father, but by me" (John 14:6). Consequently, holy living enabled by the Holy Spirit is the only way that leads to life eternal and there is no short cut. Choose this way of life and remain saved today. For" *I call heaven and earth to record this day against you, that I have set before you life and death, blessing and cursing: therefore, choose life, that both thou and thy seed may live*" (Deuteronomy 30:19).

Which way are you walking today? Is it the narrow way that leads to life everlasting or the broad way that leads to a place of punishment in Hell and destruction? Dear reader, make a right choice today by giving your life to Jesus Christ because tomorrow might be too late for you. Now is the day of salvation!

Please, email prayer requests and praise reports to:
akindewum@gmail.com

ADDENDUM

RESTORATION OF THE TREE OF LIFE

"Blessed are they that do his commandments, that they may have right to the tree of life and may enter in through the gates into the city" (Revelation 22:14).

From this verse of the Scripture, the tree of life in the book of Genesis remains in God's plan for the redeemed. It has never been forgotten. According to the book of Genesis 2:9, the tree of life was in the garden of Eden. "And the Lord God planted a garden eastward in Eden, and there he put the man whom he had formed. And out of the ground made the Lord God to grow every tree that is pleasant to the sight, and good for food; the tree of life also in the midst of the garden, and the tree of knowledge of good and evil." The tree of life is a symbol of eternal life which is the abundant life in Christ Jesus that will continue to exist forever. God is the Author of life. That is our God is the Originator and Author of natural, spiritual and eternal life. This is the full restoration of God's purpose of creation and our place in it because man, the image of God, possesses an undying soul created to live forever in God's presence in the holy city of God.

Being holy is in the sense that only the people who have given their lives to Jesus Christ and continue to overcome daily by God's available grace upon them will have access to this tree of life as described by Jesus Christ. Christ does not leave His followers comfortless and goes on to promise, "He that hath an ear, let him hear what the Spirit saith unto the churches; To him that overcometh will I give to eat of the tree of life, which is in the midst of the paradise of God" (Revelation 2:7). This promise of Paradise would encourage every Christ's follower to obey His command. What a great privilege for all believers in Christ to know that the Tree of Life, from which man was forbidden due to sin and rebellion, is once again freely accessible to those that have trusted in Christ Jesus through salvation from sin! Moreover, the leaves of the tree of life are for the healing of the nations.

In the eternal state, the curse will be no more, access to the tree of life will be reinstated and darkness will be forever banished because the unclean thing will never enter there. It is imperative for us to beware of false prophets, false apostles, false teachers and their doctrines of lukewarmness, coldness, lethargy and Nicolaitanism. Overcoming sin in one's life is the evidence of God's grace upon such a believer. To walk in the entire plan of God, man should live a life well-pleasing unto God in which he loves God and resists the sinful ways of life. Sin corrupted the original plan of God for humanity, but now, God has the plan to return it to its original state of perfection for sin to be abolished throughout all eternity. This is not possible for a man on earth without having a personal encounter with Jesus Christ in genuine salvation.

Confession of our sins, forsaking them and accepting Christ as Lord and personal Saviour by asking Him to cleanse us with His blood, opens the door to this new life. So, we continue to live and walk in the Spirit with the fruit of the Spirit (Christian's God-given behaviours – love, joy, peace, forbearance, kindness, goodness, faithfulness, gentleness and self-control from the work of the Holy Spirit in a Christian's life). In this process, we please God in absolute surrender and obedience.

Interestingly, the fruit of the Spirit come from true repentance, turning away from our sinful ways towards love for God and loving our neighbours. We endure persecution, hatred, tribulation and hardship along the narrow way that leads to eternal life. Hence, true believers qualify for Heaven by the blood of Jesus Christ that was shed for us on the cross of Calvary to live a life well-pleasing unto God here on earth before death or rapture. "She is a tree of life to them that lay hold upon her: and happy is everyone that retaineth her" (Proverbs 3:18). Due to this singular reason for victorious Christian life on earth, Paradise lost has now become Paradise regained through Christ and Satan has been beaten hands down! To God be the glory for all He has done for us through Christ by which we have the right to enter the City of New Jerusalem! Therefore, we have been given all we need for life and godliness in Christ and to know that we have a citizenship in Heaven. It is an eternal inheritance that will not fade away. We also have right to eat of the tree of life, which is in the Paradise of God!

REFERENCES

Tatford, Frederick A. (1974). *SATAN, the Prince of Darkness.* Kregel Publications, Grand Rapids, Michigan (U.S.A.)

The Holy Bible (1611). *King James Version.* Trinitarian Bible Society, England (1991). (Cambridge University Press: Cambridge)

Internet Resources:
https://en.wikipedia.org/wiki/Christian_eschatology/
https://lifeofhopeandtruth.com/
https://lifehopeandtruth.com/prophecy/end-times/surges-infectious-diseases/
https://sermons.faithlife.com/search?kinds=sermon
https://thebookofrevelationmadeclear.com/revelation-bible-study
https://www.compellingtruth.org/seven-dispensations.html
https://www.foi.org/2021/12/10/the-battle-of-gog-and-magog/
https://www.gotquestions.org/
https://www.pbs.org/wgbh/pages/frontline/shows/apocalypse/revelation/white.html
http://www.prca.org/current/Doctrine/Volume%208/news-02.htm
https://www.preceptaustin.org/messianic_prophecies

OTHER BOOKS WRITTEN
BY THE AUTHOR

1. Satanic Attacks and the Way Out
2. Victorious Christian Living Essentials
3. Prevailing Prayers of Intercession and Supplication Guides
4. Satanic Attacks and the Way Out (Second Edition)
5. Principles of Christian Marriage and Family Life
6. Evangelization and Christian Development
7. Winning the Invisible War with Christ
8. Called to be a Soldier.

These titles are available online on Amazon, Barnes & Nobles, Lulu Books, Blurb Publisher, Google play, Xlibris Publishers among others.